Regressive Illusions

Contemporary Reflections on Theory and Politics

Regressive Illusions

Contemporary Reflections on
Theory and Politics

Florian Maiwald

IFF
BOOKS

London, UK
Washington, DC, USA

CollectiveInk

First published by iff Books, 2025
iff Books is an imprint of Collective Ink Ltd.,
Unit 11, Shepperton House, 89 Shepperton Road, London, N1 3DF
office@collectiveinkbooks.com
www.collectiveinkbooks.com
www.iff-books.com

For distributor details and how to order please visit the 'Ordering' section on our website.

Text copyright: Florian Maiwald 2024

ISBN: 978 1 78099 500 7 (Paperback)
978 1 78535 990 3 (ebook)
Library of Congress Control Number: 2024952934

A CIP catalogue record for this book is available from the British Library.

Design: Lapiz Digital Services

UK: Printed and bound by CPI Group (UK) Ltd, Croydon, CR0 4YY
Printed in North America by CPI GPS partners

We operate a distinctive and ethical publishing philosophy in all areas of our business, from our global network of authors to production and worldwide distribution.

Contents

Introduction   xiii

1. "Readiness for War" and Signs of Civilizational
    Decay   1
2. Milei, Libertarian Authoritarianism and the Big
    Question of Freedom   8
3. The Regressive Illusion of Woke Capitalism   16
4. The Case of Assange: The Regressive Illusions
    Concerning Our Own Values   24
5. ChatGPT, Interpassivity and the Decay of the
    Utopian   30
6. The Regressive Illusions of the Post-Emancipatory
    Subject, or Why Chat GPT Won't Save Us   38
7. Further Reflections on Interpassivity, or the
    Outsourced Revolution   48
8. The Regressive Illusions of Jordan Peterson,
    or About a Postmodern Drinking Song   56
9. Solidarity and Its Contradictions   63
10. How to Think in the Face of Crisis?   69

Epilogue: On the Necessity of Illusions, or the
           Return of the Repressed   73
References   79

About the Author

Florian Maiwald is a German philosopher and currently teaches at the University of Bonn. He holds a PhD in Philosophy. In addition to numerous academic articles, he also publishes political articles and philosophical essays in popular media such as *Sublation Magazine*, Jacobin or ABC Australia. His book on the concept of the individual self in the works of John Stuart Mill and Erich Fromm was published by the Wissenschaftliche Buchgesellschaft (Scientific Book Society) in 2021. His book *A Socialist Liberal or a Liberal Socialist? The Value of Individuality as a Transcendence of Political Categories in the Philosophy of J.S. Mill* has been published by Nomos Publishing in May 2024.

Introduction

If one wants to grasp the current situation in which the world finds itself as adequately as possible, it is worthwhile to refer to what seems to me to be an extremely useful concept by the historian Adam Tooze: The concept of *polycrisis*. According to Tooze, the concept of polycrisis draws attention to the fact that all the challenges facing humanity in the twenty-first century – climate change, the threat of a third world war, rising global prices and the accompanying economic regression – are inextricably linked.[1] In this context, however, it is important to pay attention to Tooze's exact words regarding the definition of a polycrisis. Tooze precisely points out that "(i)n the polycrisis the shocks are disparate, but they interact so that the whole is even more overwhelming than the sum of the parts".[2] Even more interesting, however, is Tooze's conception of what qualifies as a crisis. According to Tooze, a crisis is to be understood as a progression – in the negative sense – of an original problem, in that a crisis – in contrast to an ordinary problem – calls into question our ability/possibility to cope with it and thus subsequently threatens our identity and self-image.[3]

In this way, a crisis can also be understood as the condition that Marx once formulated with clear-sightedness in his introduction to the Critique of the Hegelian Philosophy of Right when he pointed out that the demand not to have any illusions about one's own condition fails to recognise a very central aspect: the stability of the condition previously considered desirable – or rather what was generally regarded by many as normality – was itself dependent on the illusions of those people who participated in this condition, or in this form of normality.[4] In other words: The notion of an end to history, is dependent on people being under the illusion that such an end of history has actually occurred. Thus – to make a recourse to the concept of polycrisis – the current situation is characterised above all by the fact that many (especially westernised) countries are put in the situation of realising that the previous state in which they lived was also dependent on the collective illusion that we have reached the end of history. This collective illusion has led to the fact that – to formulate it with reference to Tooze's considerations – original problems that should have been addressed have advanced to crises that threaten the previous social self-understanding in many places. Or to put it another way: which have forcibly brought about the abandonment of previous illusionary thought patterns.

However, this process of disillusionment is not countered with useful and progressive social counter-strategies, but rather with what the sociologist Zygmunt Bauman once successfully called *retrotopias*: instead of looking for utopias – i.e. that future *non-place* which promises a better world – people are increasingly turning to the imagination of a supposedly lost past that is perceived as better.[5] In Marx's words: The loss of old illusionary certainties brought about by outward developments is fought with new illusions. This also seems to be a plausible explanation for why, against the backdrop of the current multiple crises confronting the world, it is not an increase in progressive visions that is gaining the upper hand, but rather regressive political forces. In my home country, Germany, the far-right party AfD (Alternative for Germany) – which is currently experiencing a frightening rise in the polls – once aptly expressed this retrotopian spirit with an election poster: "Germany. But normal."[6]

This campaign slogan of the AfD stands paradigmatically for the fact that compulsively induced forms of disillusionment are nowadays fought against in many places with more regressive and far more dangerous illusions. But what do, what I would like to call, *regressive forms of illusionary dominance* look like today?

The following – and not to mention fragmentary – reflections are meant to stimulate some thoughts regarding this question.

Regressive Illusions

In the 1960s, the US sociologist Harold Garfinkel founded the research direction of so-called ethnomethodology. The primary goal of this line of research was to show the extent to which the social structures and norms of our everyday coexistence – or rather: what we usually take for granted – depend on implicit normative prerequisites, which in turn are constituted from our everyday interactions and ultimately become routines. Using crisis experiments, Garfinkel wanted to demonstrate how fragile the norms and rules that determine our everyday lives are. For example, Garfinkel asked some of his participants not to take their products from the shelves in supermarkets, but from the shopping baskets of other customers.[7] In addition, Garfinkel asked his subjects to stand in the middle of the supermarket checkout line instead of at the end – which, of course, caused indignation on the part of other customers.

What conclusions can be drawn from Garfinkel's ethnomethodological observations? First of all, Garfinkel has been able to show very clearly the extent to which our everyday actions depend on apparent self-evident truths, which in turn depend on the (voluntary) self-deception of all those involved. The *apparent* self-evidence of these can in turn be traced back to the fact that they are of a very fragile nature. As soon as our everyday norms are confronted with a disruption, we react irritably. These irritations can be illustrated not only by everyday examples such as the wrong queue at the supermarket checkout, but also by larger political contexts – as previously illustrated with reference to Tooze's concept of polycrisis.

Don't global crises like the war in Ukraine, climate change and the Covid-19 pandemic also show that what we take for granted in our everyday lives has been disrupted? This became particularly clear with Covid-19 – a fact that Nicol A. Barria-Asenjo aptly points out in her book *Construcción de una nueva normalidad.*[8] Meeting our friends and relatives in cafés suddenly became a danger. One is also inclined to understand events like the war in Ukraine as disruptions of our everyday lives.

In this context, however, it is important not to fall prey to self-deception. If there is one important conclusion that can be drawn from Garfinkel's observations, it is above all that our everyday norms and self-evident truths are not destabilised because of some disturbance (or deviant norm) with which they are confronted, but rather because this susceptibility to disturbance is itself a direct component of the social circumstances we are confronted with.

During the Covid-19 pandemic, one of the narratives that developed was that the pandemic can be seen as a disruption of our everyday life. This statement can of course be agreed with – in part. But here we should draw the right conclusion from Garfinkel's crisis experiments and admit that this susceptibility to crisis is already an immanent part of our economic system. In this context, one is thus confronted with the question of whether the economic inequalities generated by the pandemic are to be seen as a disruption of our everyday life – which would have the consequence that any critique is constituted from the coordinates of the already existing status quo – or whether that susceptibility to crisis is not an immanent part of the system itself.

In the same way that our everyday social interactions and norms rely on our voluntary deceptions, the capitalist economic system also seems to rely on our self-deceptions. These illusions are – it can be stated at the outset – regressive in nature *since their destruction gives rise to new forms of regressive illusions.* The following essays will try to take a closer look at some of the regressive illusions of our time.

1

"Readiness for War" and Signs of Civilizational Decay

When the German Minister of Defence, Boris Pistorius, called for Germany to become ready for war again ("kriegstüchtig"), several questions arose. The most fundamental question, which one was inclined to ask immediately after Pistorius's demand, initially related to the reason for this demand. Was it to draw attention back to the Russian war of aggression against Ukraine, which is increasingly losing the focus of public attention (not least because of the reignited Middle East conflict)?

Or – and this would be an even more worrying assumption – is there actually a geopolitical potential for danger that society is not yet aware of? And was Pistorius's call for more "Kriegstüchtigkeit" ("readiness for war") a cryptic way of communicating this potential danger to the public?

The aforementioned question was not only asked by me, but – as personal conversations and the media discourse make abundantly clear – by society in general.

However, the positions are different. If one proceeds with a high degree of simplification, two main positions can be identified: one claims that Pistorius is right, and that Germany must arm itself for uncomfortable times. The other side argues that such rhetoric unnecessarily contributes to a further escalation spiral. These conflicting reactions are often characterised by the common understanding that Pistorius is primarily concerned with Germany's de facto defence capability – which is why the logical, and political, consequence must be a German military armament.

However, the much more interesting and in my opinion more important point of criticism should relate to Pistorius's choice of words and their semantic implications.

While the concept of defence capability can initially describe an objective necessity which, due to geopolitical development processes, can be achieved and implemented through clear political measures, the wording of "readiness for war" seems to imply a subjective disposition (since the capability to wage war not only requires sufficient military equipment and personnel, but also people who are willing to operate this military equipment and consequently take the risk of losing their lives for their own country). In other words: With the concept of defence capability, it could be argued quite reasonably that this is a necessary preventive measure – which, however, is initially *passive* in that it is about the *possibility* of defence (although the hope of never having to make use of this possibility should always be in the foreground).

Even though Pistorius has admitted that he can certainly understand criticism of the term "readiness for war", he has once again defended his choice of words. However, it is worth taking a closer look at Pistorius's argument.

In the ARD programme *Bericht aus Berlin*[9] (one of the main publicly funded German TV-stations) Pistorius himself admits that *readiness for war* "[...] is an ugly word for an ugly thing" and concludes that war *is* ugly.

Nevertheless, Pistorius again defends his choice of words by pointing to the need to be able to tell a potential aggressor that Germany is capable of defending itself. Pistorius continues in the light of these considerations:

And that, by the way, is the only thing that would make me angry – if someone were to accuse me of wanting to wage war. That's the last thing I want.[10]

First of all, it is interesting that Pistorius is stating the obvious here: that neither he nor the others who have a positive attitude towards the call for more "readiness for war" are in any way driven by a desire for military escalation – and indeed, it would not only be dishonest but also simply wrong to assume that Pistorius has such a motive based on his choice of words.

Nevertheless, Pistorius's attempts for justification do not in the slightest remove the problematic implications to which the term "readiness for war" leads.

First of all, the question arises as to whether a mere aggressor cannot be signalled that a military attack is not worthwhile by the sheer fact of rearmament and a drastic increase in the defence budget – because, according to the assumption, for a potential aggressor the subjective disposition to "readiness for war" is initially not visible from the outside. So even if one takes Pistorius's argumentative statements at their word, the wording of a "readiness for war" makes little sense.

However, this also reveals the far more unpleasant conclusion to which Pistorius's comments lead: Even though Pistorius acknowledges that "readiness for war" is an ugly word, he does not seem to be fully aware of *why* it is a more than problematic terminology.

Thanatos and War: Back to Freud

Against the backdrop of the sheer scale of destruction brought about by the First World War, Freud introduced the concept of the death drive (*Thanatos*) for the first time in *Beyond the Pleasure Principle*.[11] While the life instinct (*Eros*) is geared towards union, the death instinct is concerned with the dissolution of this union. To put it more concretely: the death drive's main endeavour is to come to a standstill, which manifests itself in the fact that the subject, who is permeated by the death drive, tends in particular to develop obsessive neuroses such as the compulsion to repetition (since the repetition of the same thing over and over again is ultimately based on the illusion that the existing state is maintained through constant repetition).

However, Freud's explanations are far more interesting with regard to the forms in which the death drive can occur. The subject can direct this urge to annihilation against itself (*regression*) or against other people (*aggression*).

What is more interesting, however, is when the death instinct appears in the form of aggression and is directed against others. For Freud – Freud deals with this aspect most extensively in *Society and Its Discontents*[12] – the death instinct in the form of aggression (and the accompanying desire to destroy all life) represents one of the greatest obstacles to civilized coexistence.

Einstein, Freud and the Question of War

It is worth recalling an exchange of letters between Albert Einstein and Sigmund Freud published in 1932 under the title *Why War?*[13] In this correspondence, initiated by the League of Nations, Einstein approaches Freud with the question of how humanity can be freed from the disastrous horrors of war – which of course also partially implies the question of the origins of war.

In this context, Einstein very explicitly states that he is fully aware of the fact that the predisposition for aggression – in Freudian terminology: to a death drive directed against other people – is present in every human being, even if it is only latent in times of peace:

> How is it possible that the masses can be inflamed to the point of frenzy and self-sacrifice by these means? The answer can only be: A need to hate and destroy lives in man. This disposition is latent in ordinary times and then only comes to light in the abnormal; but it can easily be awakened and increased to mass psychosis.[14]

Freud's answer to Einstein's question can of course only be reproduced here in part and in a very abbreviated form, but it is revealing in many respects. First of all, it is worth pointing out that Freud ends his answer to Einstein with the following words: "Everything that promotes the development of culture also works against war." War, understood as the death instinct, which is directed against other people in the form of aggression, can only be thwarted by the regulation of drives resulting from civilizational development processes. However, Freud becomes more specific in the previous part of his answer when he points out that the advantages resulting from human cultural development are characterised by an unmistakable form of ambivalence:

From time immemorial, the process of cultural development has dragged on over humanity. (I know, others prefer to call it civilization.) To this process we owe the best of what we have become and a good part of what we suffer from. Its origins and beginnings are obscure, its outcome uncertain, some of its characters readily apparent. [...] Perhaps this process is comparable to the domestication of certain animal species; no doubt it involves physical changes; one has not yet familiarized oneself with the idea that cultural development is such an organic process. The psychological changes that accompany the cultural process are striking and unambiguous. They consist in a progressive displacement of instinctual goals and a restriction of instinctual impulses. Sensations that were pleasurable to our ancestors have become indifferent or even disagreeable to us; there are organic reasons why our ethical and aesthetic ideals have changed.[15]

First of all, Freud points out that the process of cultural development is characterised by an unmistakable form of

5

ambivalence in that, on the one hand, modern civilizational achievements would be inconceivable without this process, but on the other hand, this process is accompanied by a high degree of suffering (Freud refers here, as also becomes clear in the passage quoted above, to the fact that it leads to a sublimation of drive goals, which in turn is itself to be regarded as a necessary prerequisite for the cultural development apostrophised by Freud and the civilizational achievements inseparably linked to it).

In the further course of his argumentation, Freud points out in an unambiguous manner that the process of sublimation – in the form of a shift in drive goals – is also accompanied by an internalization of the tendency for aggression:

> Of the psychological characteristics of culture, two seem to be the most important: the strengthening of the intellect, which begins to dominate the instincts, and the internalization of the tendency to aggression with all its beneficial and dangerous consequences. War now contradicts the psychological attitudes that the cultural process imposes on us in the most glaring way, which is why we must revolt against it, we simply can no longer tolerate it, it is not merely an intellectual and affective rejection, it is, for us pacifists, a constitutional intolerance, an idiosyncrasy, as it were, in extreme magnification. And it seems that the aesthetic humiliations of war have no less of a share in our rebellion than its atrocities.[16]

Along with the strengthening of the intellect (which Freud regards as a clearly positive aspect of cultural development), there is also a control of the instinctual life, which is initially characterised by heteronomy. When Freud points out that human cultural development contradicts the principle of war in the most fundamental way, this can be explained – and here one should read Freud as precisely as possible – by the fact that not only the fact of aggression itself – which clearly emerges in military conflicts, especially in the form of military battles – but also the *tendency to aggression* works in opposition to the general civilizational developments of humanity.

Pistorius, "Readiness for War" and the End of Civilization
If we analyse Pistorius's statements from Freud's perspective, it becomes clear at this point why Pistorius – despite his admission that "readiness for war" is an *ugly* term – does not seem to be aware of *why* it is a problematic term. Contrary to what the argument put forward by Pistorius might suggest, the concept of "readiness for war" is not the sheer fact of an objective ability to defend oneself, but rather a subjective attitude that ensures that the *tendency* to aggression is no longer subordinated to intellectual and cultural developments and therefore becomes a determining mental disposition again. This can be explained by the fact that *readiness* always requires a certain mental willingness and attitude (just as the existence of a library does not make an individual a well-read person, but also requires the inclination to want to read all the books, it also requires the ability to want to operate the corresponding military equipment).

All civilizational achievements – be it the aesthetic development of the arts, the progress of science, the struggles of the labour movement or even the mere contemplation of a better world – are based on the principle of affect regulation. Pistorius, even if he does not seem to be aware of it, has introduced a phenomenon into social discourse which threatens to negate all these achievements.

2

Milei, Libertarian Authoritarianism and the Big Question of Freedom

An interesting (or more precisely: worrying) observation can be made about the victory of Argentina's current[17] president, Javier Milei. In the so-called *villas* – a name for the slum districts in Buenos Aires – Milei won more than 30 per cent of the votes (significantly more than in the rest of the city). Milei himself has repeatedly reiterated to journalists that true liberalism is still defended in the slums – moreover, according to Milei, liberalism itself is responsible for the fact that a large part of global poverty has disappeared.

In his victory speech,[18] Milei pointed out, among other things, that Argentina was in an extremely critical and problematic situation. Against this background, Milei claimed that a drastic change is needed – and that the days of reformist gradualism are over. Milei's speech was followed by the exclamation "Liberty, liberty" and "Let them all leave" – which was of course directed at the then ruling political class (the ruling Peronist party).

First of all, it should be pointed out that traditional liberalism certainly has an emancipatory potential, which is often disregarded by many left-wing political forces – mainly against the background of the assumption that liberalism must necessarily be in contradiction to the basic socialist idea (a closer examination of authors worth reading such as Carlo Rosselli, J.S. Mill, Norberto Bobbio or the latest works by Matthew McManus show that this assumption is not correct). More interesting, however, is the question of what Milei actually means when he uses terms such as "freedom" and "liberalism".

When Milei demands in an almost revolutionary gesture that the time of gradualism is over and the rulers should step down, one is almost inclined to recognise a form of class struggle rhetoric in Milei. In this context, it is worth taking a closer look at the ideological background that shapes Milei's world view: anarcho-capitalism. First of all, anarcho-capitalism shares with other forms of anarchist theorising the fundamental insight that the state is a repressive (and therefore illegitimate) political system that restricts the freedom of society's members in an inadmissible manner. Among other things, Milei's party *La Libertad Avanza*[19] plans to completely dollarize the Argentine economy and thus undermine the welfare state (Milei announced that the number of Argentine government ministries would be reduced from 18 to 8). Milei's mixture of contradictory elements, which characterise his entire appearance, is particularly interesting: In the name of a highly abbreviated concept of freedom – which can ultimately turn into the most blatant forms of unfreedom, as the dismantling of welfare state structures, to put it polemically, ultimately only provides many people with the freedom to choose which bridge they want to sleep under – Milei often displays a thoroughly authoritarian habitus. For example, Milei often appeared at his election rallies with a chainsaw to symbolise that he would destroy the structures of the state as soon as he was in power.[20]

Milei's behaviour thus seems to be perfectly classifiable as a form of *libertarian authoritarianism* – the concept developed by Carolin Amliner and Oliver Nachtwey in their book *Gekränkte Freiheit (Offended Freedom)*,[21] published in 2022, against the backdrop of the sometimes extremely aggressive protests against the coronavirus policies at the time. The concept of libertarian authoritarianism, which Amlinger and Nachtwey develop based on the concept of authoritarianism coined by the Frankfurt School, is specifically characterised by the fact that no restrictions on individual behaviour are tolerated. This also clearly reveals the paradox of libertarian authoritarianism: the originally anarchic impulse to defend one's own freedom is enforced with a sometimes strongly authoritarian gesture. Amlinger and Nachtwey explain this paradox by pointing out that allegiance is no longer directed to a leader figure onto whom the respective authority is projected, but rather to a diffuse concept of freedom that regards any restriction of individual interests as encroaching.

Amlinger and Nachtwey express the (seemingly) contradictory elements that characterise the type of the libertarian authoritarian as follows:

> The libertarian authoritarians of our time do not primarily yearn for traditionalist values, they do not uncritically submit to leader figures. They perceive themselves as modern and thoroughly progressive, even if they are inspired by their own power and superiority. They are authoritarian insofar as they are unable to recognize either plausible values or comprehensible interests [...] in their democratic opponents.[22]

Milei seems to paradigmatically embody the type of libertarian authoritarian apostrophised by Amlinger and Nachtwey: Even if Milei is against abortions – which would violate the non-aggression principle that characterises liberalism – he expresses himself rather progressively on the subject of homosexuality[23] and gender identity and claims that it is up to each person to decide which relationship they want to enter or how they want to identify themselves. In short (Milei has also recently emphasised this point in a relatively unambiguous way): Anything that can be left to the private sector should be left to the private sector. This culminates in a claim made by Milei at a recent election campaign event[24] that it is also okay to regard one's own children as commodities that can be offered for sale on a free market. Such an understanding of freedom, which has been driven to its extreme, appears in Milei in the form of an unmistakably authoritarian gesture.

La Libertad Avanza – but Where?

One question that arises against the background of the above considerations is why Milei is able to appeal to such a high proportion of the working class (an aspect that Andrés Ruggeri and Marcelo Vieta[25] have analysed in an extremely thorough manner). First of all – and this is probably by far the most obvious point – the Left has not succeeded in politically mobilizing the discontent of large sections of Argentine society in a productive way. It goes without saying that this kind of political failure on the part of the Left is not unique to Argentina's political landscape.

A far more interesting question that arises in the context of the previous considerations relates directly to the name of Milei's party: *La Libertad Avanza* (translated: *Freedom Advances*). The right to freedom is without question an important normative foundation of today's Western democracies. However, it is also clear that freedom – understood as a condition for enabling people to do certain things – can blatantly restrict the freedom of other people or sections of the population. If Milei's party starts from the premise that freedom is advancing, this basic impetus should always be accompanied by the critical counter-question of *where* exactly this freedom is advancing. In other words: The use of freedom can also turn into entirely new forms of barbarism and unfreedom. Against the backdrop of their development of the concept of libertarian authoritarianism, Amlinger and Nachtwey point out that the concept of freedom that libertarian authoritarians advocate today is different from the emancipatory aspirations that drove both the bourgeoisie and the labour movement.[26] While the bourgeoisie's and the workers' movements' aspirations for freedom revolved around an increased degree of participation (and thus also equality) by declaring war on outdated feudal structures or unjust economic conditions, today's libertarian understanding of freedom is characterised specifically by the fact that fundamental social agreements, which are a necessary prerequisite for the freedom of all, are subjected to radical questioning as soon as they threaten to restrict the freedom of the individual. However, restrictions can already be understood here as basic civilizational self-evident truths (such as paying taxes or medical protective measures that serve the common good of society).

While Erich Fromm argued – not least in his great work *Escape from Freedom* – that the authoritarianism that emerged in the Third Reich was characterised by a fear of freedom, the ideology underlying Milei's world view is specifically characterised by the fact that the idea of freedom is taken to its extreme consequences – and thus paradoxically abolishes itself. The freedom to which Milei's party ultimately wishes to progress in accordance with its name appears to be a form of pseudo-freedom insofar as it negates a very basic idea, which is ultimately to be regarded as constitutive for the practical realisation of a concept of freedom that deserves its name: that real freedom can only be realised within specific social structures.

Abstract and Concrete Freedom

In his book *Freedom: A Disease Without Cure,*[27] Slavoj Žižek draws on the Hegelian difference between abstract and concrete freedom. While abstract freedom is characterised by the fact that the subject transcends all social rules and customs in his own actions and can consequently do as he/she pleases, concrete freedom cannot be conceived without the prevailing social and normative background conditions. In this regard, Žižek writes that "concrete freedom" is the freedom located within and sustained by a set of social rules and customs. With regard to anti-vaxxers in the Covid pandemic, the freedom to choose being vaccinated or not is of course a formal kind of freedom; however, to reject vaccination effectively implies limiting my actual freedom as well as the freedom of others. Within a community, being vaccinated means I am a much lesser threat to others (and others to me), so I can to a much greater degree exercise my social freedoms to mix with others in the usual way. My freedom is only actual as freedom within a certain social space regulated by rules and prohibitions. I can walk freely along a busy street because I can be reasonably sure that others on the street will behave in a civilized way towards me, will be punished if they attack me, if they insult me, etc. – and it is exactly the same with vaccination. Of course, we can strive to change the rules of common life – there are situations when these rules can be relaxed, but also strengthened (as in the conditions of a pandemic), but a domain of rules is needed as the very terrain of our freedoms.[28]

According to Žižek, the (apparent) paradox of the concept of freedom lies precisely in the fact (as becomes more than clear when the Hegelian difference between abstract and concrete freedom is brought to mind) that the exercise of concrete freedom can only be fully realised against the background of specific rules and prohibitions – which, of course, conversely means that the concrete, i.e. practical realisation of freedom is often dependent on the loss (or limitation) of abstract forms of freedom. Thus, the decision to be vaccinated or not can initially be recognised as an abstract form of freedom. However, abstract freedom is subject to considerable restrictions in its concrete form, as it fails to recognise that as an individual you are always embedded in social structures and that such a decision can endanger the health and well-being of other members of society. Similarly, social freedom of movement (understood as a very concrete freedom that every citizen should enjoy) is only possible against the background of the implicit normative assumption that one should not attack other people – so that they in turn can stroll through the city centre without worrying. Or, to cite another example: The freedom (which most people take for granted) to eat in a restaurant during their lunch break is (I) dependent on the financial resources to be able to pay for the meal in question and (II) – to use a somewhat exaggerated example – that one can assume that the restaurant staff will not make use of their abstract freedom to poison the meal in question.

According to Žižek, the Hegelian difference between abstract and concrete freedom can also be illustrated using the example of language. Initially, the use of language also represents an unmistakable form of freedom, as it enables people to communicate with others – furthermore, state structures and political agreements would not even be conceivable without such contexts of interaction. However, the freedom to enter a linguistic form of interaction with other people also depends on certain conditions. For example, the person who intends to use a certain language must observe the syntactic rules that make any form of linguistic communication possible in the first place. Nevertheless, such observance of syntactic rules is only a necessary, but not a sufficient condition for the concrete freedom to make use of language (in a meaningful way). Žižek also clearly points out that the successful use of language also implies mastering semantics – including its contradictory and ambiguous elements:

> I can only exert this freedom if I obey the commonly
> established rules of language (with all their ambiguities
> and inclusive of the unwritten rules of messages between

the lines). What a society in its public discourse doesn't find satisfying is its specific repressed-unwritten rules, obscene supplements which are socially not recognized but necessary.[29]

Returning to Milei's concept of human freedom, the chainsaw with which Milei constantly appeared during his campaign events symbolically stands for nothing less than the endeavour to destroy the conditions that are a prerequisite for the practice of concrete freedom. The Hegelian differentiation between abstract and concrete freedom cited by Žižek also serves as an extremely helpful approach for explaining why the type of libertarian authoritarian apostrophised by Amlinger and Nachtwey – of which Milei is to be seen as a paradigmatic example – is by no means characterised by contradictory ideological interpretations of the world: The very ignorance of the concrete – understood as the moral/societal agreements – in favour of the supposed right to practise abstract freedoms, ultimately leads to the destruction of the possibility of making use of concrete freedoms at all. This is the world that Milei has in mind – a world in which the only freedom that people really have is the freedom to choose under which bridge they want to sleep when they haven't made it at the end of the day.

3

The Regressive Illusion of Woke Capitalism[1]

With regard to Donald Trump's 2016 election victory, Nancy Fraser aptly pointed out that this victory – and populist tendencies in general – cannot be attributed solely to neoliberal developments in the economic sphere. Rather, according to Fraser, it is precisely these economic developments with a (false) progressive flavour (more specifically: progressive neoliberalism) that has frightened off many of Trump's supporters. According to Fraser, progressive neoliberalism is specifically characterised by the fact that it represents an alliance "[...] of mainstream currents of new social movements (feminism, anti-racism, multiculturalism, and LGBTQ rights), on the one side, and high-end 'symbolic' and service-based business sectors (Wall Street, Silicon Valley, and Hollywood), on the other".[30] According to Fraser, this unique alliance is characterised by the fact that neoliberal structural measures could be implemented in an emancipatory guise. Recently, authors such as Cathrine Liu have also subsumed this alliance of progressive values and capital under the term professional-managerial class (PMC).[31]

However, if one takes a closer look at this phenomenon – or rather concept – also often labelled as *woke capitalism*, certain ideological contradictions emerge. These contradictions can be illustrated by the internet giant Amazon, which boasts with pathos about the diversity of its own company:

---

1   This article was previously published by Everyday Analysis.

Amazon has hundreds of millions of customers who benefit from the diversity of our thinking: Our company is made up of doers who bring their diverse backgrounds, ideas and perspectives to our innovations. Our diversity comes from characteristics such as gender, ethnic background, culture and nationality, age, sexual orientation and education, but also professional and personal experience. We want to develop leaders and meet the needs of Amazon's customers from around the world. We are growing – and embracing a culture of difference. At the same time, we are working to continuously increase the proportion of women employed.[32]

Furthermore, the internet giant particularly emphasises the promotion of diversity through its *Glamazon* project:

As an official affinity group, an association of like-minded employees, GLAmazon advocates for the LGBTQ community (lesbian, gay, bisexual, trans, queer) at Amazon. Their goal: to promote an open and tolerant working environment that supports equal opportunities and activates talent. Glamazon is not only involved internally, for example, by organising networking meetings to get to know each other. Glamazon is also active outside the company. In the context of the debate on marriage for all, the group supported the campaign "For all who say yes now" last year.[33]

As laudable and important as these demands are, the question remains whether they are not in blatant contradiction to the systematic intimidation of trade union demands that Amazon continually engages in. It has become known – especially in the US – that Amazon hires so-called *union busters* who ensure that the trade unions are kept as weak and small as possible.[34]

The example of Amazon, however, is only one example among many.

According to this logic, the disruptions that shape our social coexistence – racism, sexism, etc. – can only be solved within the coordinates of the existing system. Or to put it another way: the logic, which likely can even be seen (at least in part) as the cause of those social problems, such as sexism, racism etc., now presents itself not as part of, but as the key to solving those problems. Consequently, according to this view, only the current economic system itself can solve those problems (for which, however, it itself is in many ways partly responsible). To preserve its own survival, the economic structures depend on the self-deception of all those involved: social antagonisms, such as sexism, racism, and the unequal distribution of wealth, are disruptive factors that can be remedied through appropriate approaches to solutions within the coordinates of the current economic logic.

The phenomenon of *woke capitalism* primarily refers to the (quite economically motivated) efforts of large corporations to instrumentalise the demands of progressive movements – such as those of Black Lives Matter or the LGBTQ+ movement – for their own corporate purposes. The primary origin of this instrumentalization of progressive demands, however, cannot be traced back to the fact that the respective companies share those progressive demands, but rather to the fact that this publicly postulated (apparent) solidarity serves their own profit interests. As a result of these hypocritical declarations of solidarity by big companies, progressive demands are depoliticised and deprived of their emancipatory substance. In an article in *The Guardian*, Owen Jones clairvoyantly introduced the term *woke washing* in this context (in reference to the term *greenwashing*).[35]

Against the background of these considerations, it seems almost absurd to speak of an awakened capitalism that claims to have "woken up" and to have seen through the systemic structures that are responsible for the suffering and poverty in our world. Paradoxically, the ideology of capitalist *wokeness* is itself part of the dogmatic slumber – to apply a term of Immanuel Kant to another context – on whose continuation the stability of the economic structures depends for their own reproduction.

Carl Rhodes aptly sums up the basic problem of a capitalism that claims to be awakened:

> If awakening capitalism has achieved anything, it has been to break the yoke between social and economic policy that has traditionally united the right. This means that companies can support social justice without worrying about its inescapable relationship to economic justice. If CEOs want to pursue progressive policies, they must also support raising the minimum wage, introducing a universal basic income, redistributing income through higher taxes on the rich, and guaranteeing workers' rights through trade unions. The worst part is that when CEOs are condemned as left-wing nutcases, their political activism diverts attention from the core political problem of economic inequality – the very inequality that too many CEOs represent.[36]

The instrumentalization of progressive demands by big corporations ultimately ensures that they present themselves as "awakened" and avoid the important economic demands – redistribution of income, higher taxes for the rich, strengthening of trade unions, etc. A real awakening from the dogmatic slumber would be accompanied by the realisation that a truly progressive corporate policy does not further contribute to these forms of social depoliticisation but turns to precisely those core materialist problems.

The Pursuit of (Un)Happiness: The Neoliberal Way of Life
At this point it is worth returning to Marx's thoughts from the introduction to the *Critique of the Hegelian Philosophy of Right*.[37]

What would it mean to free oneself from the illusion of neoliberal capitalism – which, with polemical exaggeration, can perhaps already be seen as a kind of substitute religion for human beings?

Perhaps a real awakening would be accompanied by the realisation that the functioning or reproducibility of the neoliberal-capitalist economic system also depends on our illusions. Moreover, it is perhaps worth going even further than Marx himself at this point: The abolition of the capitalist economic system as the illusory happiness of people may not even necessarily result in people achieving their real happiness. Is not the concept of happiness itself to be regarded as an immanent component of capitalist ideology? This becomes clear not least from the core idea of the American Way of Life, which assumes that everyone in the capitalist economic system has the possibility to strive for and achieve their own happiness – if they only work hard enough for it. One of the most common – and justified – criticisms of this idea is that failure in personal advancement is always due to an individual rather than a systemic failure. The film *The Pursuit of Happiness*, released in 2006, can be seen as a paradigmatic example of this same ideological stance: The film centres on single father Chris Gardner (played by Will Smith), who is abandoned by his wife due to permanent financial difficulties. Firmly committed to giving his son a better life, Gardner eventually manages – after some extremely tragic stops in between (including homelessness) – to get a job at a successful investment bank. The basic idea is, of course, relatively clear: if you work hard enough, you'll make it. And if you don't, then you didn't work hard enough (imagine a Hollywood film in which Gardner didn't make it in the end. What conclusions would people then be prepared to draw?). The film itself is paradigmatic for the *survivorship bias*, which is particularly common in discourses about economic justice: Due to a cognitive bias, we assume that achieving success is not that unlikely, since our perceptual radar is usually only focused on the (few) people who have been successful – as opposed to the many less successful people who have not.[38] At this point, however, the question remains whether the basic idea of the individual pursuit of happiness (and the possibility of achieving happiness through hard work) should not also be criticised from a completely different perspective: Is not perhaps even the concept of happiness itself to be doubted? Can we not rather assume that the idea of happiness itself only endures through its own unattainability? In other words, only the unattainability of happiness ensures that people remain willing to strive for a (non-existent) state of perfect happiness (which, of course, they will never achieve). It seems quite plausible to assume that this de facto unattainability of happiness is a basic driver of the capitalist pursuit of competition. Neoliberal capitalism thus thrives on our own self-deception that we are responsible for our own happiness. Thus, thinkers such as Julie Reshe have repeatedly and correctly pointed out that the concept of happiness itself should be radically questioned – not least because happiness makes it impossible for people to face reality, which is a necessary prerequisite for achieving any sort of systemic change.[39] Capitalism cannot ultimately be *woke*, only we ourselves can be. To really wake up would mean to realise to what extent the reproduction of capitalist structures depends on our own (illusory) beliefs.

The Capitalist Unconscious

Erich Fromm once aptly pointed out – following Freud's concept of the unconscious – that in addition to the individual unconscious areas of repression, there is also a social unconscious that denotes those areas of repression, which are found in most members of a society. These elements, repressed by the general public, are contents that the members of the respective society must not become aware of if this society with its specific contradictions is to function smoothly.[40]

Following Fromm, it also seems plausible to assume that in addition to the social unconscious, there is also a capitalist unconscious, which, however, cannot be understood as a secondary category, but rather as a subcategory of the social unconscious. Our economic system, with all its contradictions, ultimately also depends on our repressions and the resulting self-deceptions to continue to function smoothly. We develop rationalisations to conceal these specific contradictions. Insecure employment contracts and the compulsion to constantly reorient oneself professionally are consequently translated as the possibility of freedom and self-realisation. Or big capitalist companies present themselves as the big problem solvers of social problems like sexism and racist discrimination – and at the same time make sure that we suppress the fact that the exploitative conditions of these companies are perhaps even the origin of many of these problems.

One of the main challenges seems to be to bring those areas of the capitalist unconscious to consciousness. This would amount to a real awakening. In addition, we must face a fact – albeit an unpleasant one – that concerns the core of our human self-understanding: we are masters of self-deception! We are increasingly afflicted by weather extremes such as heatwaves and floods, yet we continue to eat too much meat and jet around the globe on cheap flights.

What is at work here seems to remain an unsolved riddle on a philosophical level: While we are capable of the highest insights on an abstract level, in the concreteness of our existence we manage to constantly act contrary to these insights.

Perhaps – and I am aware that this is a very provocative thought – it is a necessary condition for the translation of abstract insight into concrete action that the objective coordinates of the crisis encounter the subjective coordinates of our existence. Perhaps we would then be able to come to the realisation that an ecological transformation of our economic system should not be at the expense of the weak and poor, but that a continuation of the status quo will lead to far greater social divisions. Perhaps we would then come to the realisation that being truly *woke* means recognising that the neoliberal economic system is not the solution, but part of our social problems. It is indeed time to wake up. But properly!

4

The Case of Assange: The Regressive Illusions Concerning Our Own Values[2]

June 17, 2022, was indeed a more than tragic day for the Western world. The British government has agreed to extradite Julian Assange to the United States, where he now faces 175 years in prison for journalistic disclosure of war crimes. Background: via the disclosure platform Wikileaks, Assange published, among other things, the video "Collateral Murder", in which the shooting of unarmed Iraqi civilians from a US military helicopter is documented.[41] The consequence: after the Ecuadorian embassy in London no longer granted Assange refuge, he had already been in the London high-security prison Belmarsh, which according to some statements resembles a "British Guantanamo", for months. There Assange stays under inhumane conditions and lives 23 hours a day in complete isolation.

All of this seems even more paradoxical against the background of the fact that Assange is not even a US citizen – he is Australian – and has committed none of his alleged crimes on US soil. The statements of former CIA director Leon Panetta[42] should make us think even more when he points out that the US is primarily interested in making an example regarding the Assange case. In concrete terms, this means as much as that every investigative journalist who intends to bring war crimes by the US army to the public's attention must expect a similar punishment in the future. The Assange case makes it absolutely

---

2   This article was previously published by *Sublation Magazine*. Slight reformulations have been made. This article has been written before Assange has been
released from Belmarsh.

clear that it is not just about the future of Assange in particular, but about the future of freedom of the press and freedom of expression in general, and thus, to some extent, about the future of all of us.

However, the Assange case should not be seen as an isolated individual case. Especially with regard to the current global political situation, which has changed dramatically – not least due to Putin's criminal war of aggression against Ukraine – the Assange case could provide important lessons for the so-called Western world, which always claims to defend its own liberal-democratic values against the worldwide increase in autocratic tendencies. The war of aggression launched by Putin against Ukraine has made us painfully aware that there are forces in the world that perceive liberal democracies as a threat. It is therefore consistent and logical to try to protect ourselves against such external threats in the most expedient way possible.

On Western Contradictions

What the Assange case shows, however, is that it is a mistake to assume that the threat to democratic ways of life can only be attributed to external factors (autocracies, etc.). Rather, as the Assange case makes abundantly clear, such a threat for – or more concretely, destabilisation of – democratic structures can also be caused by democracies themselves. It is Assange's achievement to have relentlessly brought this aspect to our attention.

With his concept of the social character, Erich Fromm described a phenomenon that is supposed to explain to what extent there is a social unconscious in addition to the psychological unconscious in the Freudian sense. Here it is worth citing Fromm:

The social character, which causes people to act and think as the proper functioning of their social life requires, is

25

only one link between social structure and ideas. The other link is the fact that each society determines which thoughts may enter consciousness and which must remain unconscious.[43]

While the social character is oriented towards actions and thoughts that lead to a reproduction of the existing social conditions, the social unconscious describes the repression that is necessary in order that this very reproduction of the social conditions will not be disturbed. Applying Fromm's thoughts to the case of Assange, the following becomes clear:

Unconsciously, it may have been obvious to us for some time that the narrative of freedom characteristic of the Western world is marked by a certain ambivalence – we rightly condemn Russia's or China's treatment of their own journalists, but doesn't the US do the same thing when it wants to lock up a journalist who brought war crimes to the public's attention? It is precisely those ambivalences that have been brought to light by the Wikileaks revelations and which have led to a disruption of the existing social narrative. Assange has brought to consciousness what we were not allowed to become aware of and is now to be punished for it. He has ensured an end to the world as we previously perceived it (or should have perceived it). Assange has exposed what we currently rightly condemn about Russia's war of aggression: the pointless killing of civilians (which cannot ever be reasonable under any conceivable context) through war crimes.

A Global Turning Point

In order to understand what the Assange case means in concrete terms one should first realise that we are indeed currently living through a turning point in time (in German: *Zeitenwende*) – as German Chancellor Scholz rightly affirms over and over again.

We are living in an age of multiple crises, which – as Colombia's former Finance Minister Mauricio Cárdenas[44] rightly points out – cannot be viewed in isolation from one another. Catastrophes such as the increasingly extreme climate crisis, the Covid-19 pandemic as well as the intensifying famines caused by war make it clear that the crises, we are facing cannot be solved within a nation-state framework but can only be managed through new forms of global solidarity in the form of cross-state cooperation. The measures that may have to be employed to solve these problems may seem radical, as they challenge some of the basic premises of the current global capitalist system. Nevertheless, it should be kept in mind that the crises we are facing on a global scale (and some of which have already hit us!) are also radical, which is why the measures needed to tackle these crises – in line with the etymological origin of the concept of radicality – must go to the root of the problems.

At this point, one may legitimately ask what the Assange case has to do with the lines of thought mentioned here regarding the management of global crises.

At the Globesec 2022 Forum in Bratislava, Indian Foreign Minister Subrahmanyam Jaishankar responded to the accusation of why India was still buying Russian oil as follows:

> Europe has to grow out of the mindset that its problems are the world's problems, but the world's problems are not Europe's problems. [...] There is a lot happening outside Europe. There are so many human and natural disasters in our part of the world, and many countries are asking India for help. The world is changing, and new actors are coming in. The world can no longer be Eurocentric. [...] Tell me that buying Russian gas is not financing the war? It is only Indian money that finances the war, not the gas that flows to Europe.[45]

Jaishankar points out the important aspect that successful management of the global crises that await us in fact requires that we recognise that our perceptions of geopolitical crises cannot be considered representative of the global perceptions of those very crises. The problems that await us can no longer be seen as intra- or extra-European. Already in the Covid-19 pandemic, this problem of a Western (though not necessarily intentional) double standard has become apparent when it came to the globally equitable distribution of vaccines. Mike Ryan, head of the WHO's Global Health Crisis Programme, for example, has pointed out the following:

> The rich countries have decided to vaccinate the entire adult population first and only then deal with global distribution. And now, booster vaccinations of their own populations are more important to them than the initial vaccinations of the most vulnerable people in poor countries. When that is done, the children will come. Then it will be more important to vaccinate five- to twelve-year-olds than high-risk patients on the other side of the world. So when, in God's name, are we going to have a discussion about equity and the most effective use of this vaccine? It remains a tragedy.[46]

While there has been talk within some societies about the solidarity of getting vaccinated, the global scope of the whole problem has been completely ignored. But it is not only at the level of globally equitable vaccine distribution that this problem becomes apparent. The breakdown in supply chains already caused by the pandemic, and the food shortages that accompany it, will be dramatically intensified by the war, especially in developing countries.

Mohamed A EL-Erian[47] aptly sums up the entire issue when he points out that we are currently dealing with multiple "little fires" that will ruin the already economically destabilised developing countries. We can only put out these fires if we show the same commitment to these global problems that we are showing in the Ukraine war. We must not only show that we can live up to the visions of a peaceful Western world that are driving the flight and resistance of the Ukrainian people in the facticity of our actions. We must also understand that beyond this, our task is to show the world that democracies are the stronger system in the long run than Putin's autocratic regime.

However, we can only succeed in this if we realise that other countries are watching us very closely. If we condemn Putin's war of aggression (rightly!) in the strongest terms, we cannot at the same time lock up those who have brought to light the war crimes committed by the West. We cannot blame other countries like India – which has gone through a heatwave that has brought the loss of several lives – for perceiving global issues in a different way than we do. Heatwaves in India are to be considered our problem in the same way as floods in the Ahr Valley. Famines in developing countries are to be seen as our problem in the same way as the increase in precarious conditions in our own countries. We should condemn the fact that disclosure of war crimes in the Western world is punishable by 175 years in prison in the same way as when dissidents in Russia or China are locked up for opposing the official state ideology. We should condemn the killing of Iraqi civilians, made public by the Wikileaks revelations, in the same way as we condemn the horrific massacres in Bucha. Assange has shown that we can only claim to postulate our values on a global scale if we act in coherent accordance with those very values. Are we ready to defend Assange's emancipatory legacy by finally learning to live up to our own values without contradictions?

ChatGPT, Interpassivity and the Decay of the Utopian[3]

It's a rainy afternoon and I'm bored. In other words, postponing things that I really should be doing. What could be more appealing in such a moment than playing around with ChatGPT?

For a long time, I have been thinking about writing an essay concerning the usefulness of "whataboutism" – an argumentative strategy in which a critical objection is not discussed but answered with a critical counter-objection. Especially now, in times of the war in Ukraine, the argument that not only Russia but also the West has committed numerous war crimes is often branded as a "whataboutism". The argument (very crudely broken down) is that one wrong is not undone by another wrong. Applied concretely in terms of the current situation: even if the Iraq war was absolutely illegitimate from the perspective of international law, that still does not by any means justify Putin's war of aggression in Ukraine.

Of course, this criticism is absolutely justified from an ethical point of view. However, for some time now I have been asking myself whether the use of "whataboutism" as an argumentative strategy – depending on the intention with which it is used – can also have some strengths.

With these considerations in mind, I asked ChatGPT to write a critical essay – out of sheer experimentation, of course, and never with the intention, this note is important, of considering it a serious work product – which was to be a plea for the argumentative strategy of "whataboutism".

---

3   This article was previously published by *Sublation Magazine*. Slight reformulations have been made.

The result was sobering in many ways, and also one of the central reasons why my fear that ChatGPT might replace the human capacity for creativity and intellectual reflection was somewhat muted. The chatbot's response was that it was not possible to write an essay on the strengths of "whataboutism". However, after this preliminary remark, I received a long essay on defining "whataboutism" and, in a second step, why this argumentative strategy should be considered highly questionable.

At this point, it is by no means my intention to write a plea for "whataboutism" – this project is still on my personal to-do list. Let me just say this: There are good arguments for the contextual use of "whataboutism". The US-American philosopher Ben Burgis draws attention to this fact very aptly:

> But if you aren't at least asking the "what about...?" questions, you simply aren't serious about applying morally consistent standards. Waxing indignant about the misdeeds of other powers while refusing to look in the mirror is what Vladimir Putin does when he simultaneously condemns American imperialism and wages war to keep a less powerful neighbor in his country's sphere of influence. Let's be better than that.[48]

If one applies Burgis's argument to the current global and political situation, especially against the background of the war in Ukraine, it becomes clear that the argumentative strategy of "whataboutism" and its justification depend to a considerable extent on the intention with which one uses it. If this argument is only used to justify Putin's war of aggression (according to the motto: "We should rather be quiet, because the Western NATO countries have also committed several war crimes"), then this criticism of the "whataboutism" line of argumentation is more than justified. Not least because Putin's war of aggression is solely his fault.

The argument Burgis develops, however, accurately draws attention to the fact that the use of "whataboutism" can also empower human beings – or governments – to practise self-criticism. In times of increasing militarization, both in discursive and real political relations, which is justified by the defence of human rights, it is therefore quite useful to recall that Julian Assange might have faced 175 years of prison in the US for journalistic exposure of war crimes. Or that the Guantánamo prison camp still exists.

The Limitations of ChatGPT

ChatGPT would not acknowledge this fact on that rainy Sunday afternoon when I was bored and interacting with the chatbot. This identifies one of ChatGPT's core problems, which is actually the point of this article: The personal identification of socio-political grievances – a central prerequisite for any form of active political participation – is delegated to a system whose output is shaped by algorithmic calculations, thus letting the political potential inherent in many forms of creativity and critical engagements with the world succumb to passivity.

In this context, the US video game designer Ian Bogost aptly points out why ChatGPT is precisely not to be regarded as a system that can replace human creativity and an accompanying creative power:

> Computers have never been instruments of reason that can solve matters of human concern; they're just apparatuses that structure human experience through a very particular, extremely powerful method of symbol manipulation. That makes them aesthetic objects as much as functional ones. GPT and its cousins offer an opportunity to take them up on the offer—to use computers not to carry out tasks but to mess around with the world they have created. Or better: to destroy it.[49]

32

This news is of course comforting insofar as it makes it clear that fears of algorithms being able to completely replace human thinking and creative powers one day would be pointless. However – as has already been pointed out to some extent – the danger of such systems is that they create a form of passivity that makes any form of active political power, which is a basic prerequisite for social change on a large scale, impossible. In contrast to human beings, chatbots are not a representation of human reason, which is capable of critically reflecting the social conditions by which human beings are surrounded. If one realises that the software developed by OpenAI is nothing more than that, we have nothing to fear. Rather, the danger is that we will reach a point where we understand ChatGPT as more than just an algorithm-based interaction engine perfectly capable of structuring the conglomeration of human experience through the manipulation of symbols.

More concretely: The danger is that we begin to impute some form of reason to such software, even though we are aware that it is incapable of reasoned thought. In other words, if we no longer confront such software on an interactive level, but on what the philosopher Robert Pfaller calls an *interpassive* level.

ChatGPT and Interpassivity

Interactivity would still imply that both the bot and the person operating the chatbot are actively involved in the process. To return to the example mentioned at the beginning: While the activity of ChatGPT concretely consisted in implementing my request to write an essay about the positive aspects regarding "whataboutism" by means of manipulating symbols of various algorithms, my activity – and thus my reflective thought processes – finally consisted in recognizing that the bot was not capable of doing so and thus was not suitable as an expressive instrument of genuine political will formation. With interpassivity, however, it is a different matter.

About the concept of interpassivity, Robert Pfaller writes:

> Interpassivity is the case when somebody prefers to delegate their enjoyment (their passivity) to some other instead of enjoying themselves [...]. To give an example, I once encountered a man who was a big drinker. All of a sudden he changed, and did not drink any more. But he adopted a new passion: he became a perfect host. He would always have a bottle in his hand and take care that the glasses of his guests were refilled, so that he could, as it were, continue to be a drinker through his guests. He had become an interpassive drinker.[50]

According to Pfaller, it is crucial that this process of delegating one's own enjoyment consists in the fact that the corresponding actor does not have to enjoy his object of pleasure (the glass of wine, the pizza, the cigarette, etc.) him/herself, but delegates it to another actor who carries out the process of enjoyment for him/her. Pfaller's concept of interpassivity can also be used to clarify precisely where the concrete dangers of ChatGPT lie. Even if Pfaller, especially in later works, is primarily concerned with the delegation of human enjoyment to a second instance – Pfaller also cites the example of a customer at a bar who orders a beer, pays for it, but lets another customer drink the beer – Pfaller's thoughts can also be easily applied to political contexts by replacing the notion of enjoyment with the notion of creativity (even if one can indeed argue about whether creativity and enjoyment, at least partially, cannot also be inseparably linked). Creativity has always been a necessary ingredient not only for artistic excellence, but also for being able to imagine alternative conceptions of society and, inextricably linked to it, to initiate political change.

Zygmunt Bauman once said that utopias are capable of relativising the present. Bauman then goes on to say:

By exposing the partiality of current reality, by scanning the field of the possible in which the real occupies merely a tiny plot, utopias pave the way for a critical attitude and a critical activity which alone can transform the present predicament of man. The presence of a utopia, the ability to think of alternative solutions to the festering problems of the present, may be seen therefore as a necessary condition of historical change.[51]

The ability to think of alternative solutions for the problems of the present, which is inseparably connected with the imagination of utopian conceptions of society, is not only – to use Stéphane Hessel's expression – connected with the ability to outrage, but also with the ability to think creatively, in order to be able to react to the outrage provoking grievances, which one finds, in a manner which in the long run contributes to the development of solutions which are able to eliminate the corresponding problems. Or formulated differently: To get from the actual state characterised by the social problems one finds oneself surrounded by to a target state which seems utopian. ChatGPT is not capable of that critical attitude and the associated activity of which Bauman speaks.

Thus it was precisely the impoverishment of the proletariat set in motion by the industrial development processes that induced Marx – with constant help from Engels – to write *Capital* in order to give expression to his own indignation and thus also to his own attitude towards these conditions in a creative and, from an intellectual point of view, eloquent manner and to mobilise politically generations of human beings in both positive and negative ways.

The Destruction of Emancipatory Creativity

ChatGPT threatens to destroy this creative potential in human beings which is the prerequisite for social change. The worries that students and pupils will fall prey to convenience and hand in mediocre work due to ChatGPT are absolutely justified from the point of view of intellectual emancipation – even if ChatGPT does not seem to be able to produce even rudimentarily acceptable results at the moment, mainly due to its strongly formalistic structure. However, the analysis should go much further at this point and our concerns should go much deeper: Should ChatGPT really ensure that human beings at a certain point no longer merely interact with this AI system, but enter into a relationship of interpassivity, it could be that we enter a state of society in which human beings no longer function as emancipatory actors capable of initiating sociopolitical change.

We may not (necessarily) delegate our pleasure to a chatbot, but we may delegate our imagination and creativity by transferring the actual human ability to interpret the world to an AI system. Of course, one might argue that these are all too dystopian scenarios, as most human beings are well aware of the limitations of such a system. On the other hand, exactly therein lies the danger that one delegates one's own creative potential of interpreting the world to an AI, knowing that its implementation is subject to strong limitations. Avantika Tewari makes it very clear that this form of an interpassive relationship is possible, regardless of the limitations of ChatGPT:

> In order for humans to believe in the power of artificial intelligence they must learn to believe in it despite its own limits with all its factual inaccuracies, inconsistencies and blurriness. It is only when our human subjectivity is inscribed to ChatGPT – with our own gaze by catching its glitches and mistakes – that the system breathes life [...]. In fact, the very limit of the AI forms the contour of our consciousness, retrospectively. We know the system cannot outsmart us yet we want to battle it out with our wits to better its capacity to fight us.[52]

Of course, Tewari already hints at the dystopian scenario that ChatGPT might one day be able to outsmart human beings. Much more worrying, however, is the fact that human beings delegate their creative potential to an AI, knowing full well that the latter is characterised by limitations and that they derive pleasure from precisely this circumstance. What if Marx would have had *Capital* written by a sophisticated AI system that boasts phrases like, "Even though neoliberal capitalism produces inconceivable amounts of poverty, it is nevertheless the best of all systems." And what if Marx had been content with that and then just gone to the pub around the corner ordering a beer – to be consumed by another guest? I don't know exactly, of course. But what I do know for sure is that I would not want to live in such a world. In short, we should (to use Freud's words) stand by our political id, which longs for the enjoyment of a politically more just society, instead of being constantly bullied by our political superego, which wants us to believe that imagining alternative ways of organizing society that are characterised by more justice is to be regarded as something sinful. If we do not want to follow this political superego, we should also not follow everything that a bot tells us.

6

The Regressive Illusions of the Post-Emancipatory Subject, or Why Chat GPT Won't Save Us[4]

In his more than underrated work – which should be required reading for anyone committed to leftist theorising – *Socialismo Liberale*, Italian publicist and politician Carlo Rosselli (1899–1937) poses a bold thesis that may be considered provocative: Against the background of the rising fascism in Italy and the incapacity of the socialist movement that was becoming apparent at that time, Rosselli asks whether historical materialism does not rather benefit the capitalist class than the workers' movement itself. This paradoxical situation, which according to this reading is to be regarded as constitutive for the crisis of the Marxist movement at that time, is impressively presented by Rosselli:

> The capitalist, particularly the entrepreneur, being in charge of the production process, dominating and linking its elements, sharing actively in technical progress, possesses an awareness of his active participation in the transformation of the process of production. He is able concretely to insert his will into history, and his relation to economic life is typically one of action-reaction. The proletarian (and the intellectual who joins the cause of the workers on his behalf), however, since he only feels the effects or is forced to assist passively in the process of production, sees the forces of production merely as controlling factors against which, at present,

---

4   This article was previously published by *Sublation Magazine*. Slight reformulations have been made.

he is powerless to react. Historical materialism, when he applies it, becomes not a liberating philosophy but a philosophy that shows him his chains, and in doing so induces him to make vain attempts to get free of them.[53]

When Rosselli points out that historical materialism does not liberate workers from their chains – created by the capitalist system of production – he makes a case for a form of voluntarism that is otherwise only found in the libertarian spectrum. The labour movement needs a new philosophy in which it sees itself as an active emancipatory actor and not as a passive victim of the prevailing social conditions. Against the background of these considerations, Rosselli comes to the insight that "[...] (t)he concrete historical process, as the devotees of historical materialism have depicted it, is history lived by nobody, history a posteriori, history for professors. Its vaunted compass works only after the ship is in port".[54]

Even though Rosselli's work, which he wrote in 1923 during his exile on the island of Lipari, boils down to the impressive thesis that socialism must regain awareness of its liberal essence, I would like to use the previously quoted passage to focus on a different problem: If Rosselli laments at the time that historical materialism benefits the class of capitalists rather than the working class, this situation can be captured by the concept of *interpassivity* coined later by philosophers such as Robert Pfaller and Slavoj Žižek. Even though Pfaller clearly points out that the concept of interpassivity is concretely characterised by the delegation of one's own pleasure (or enjoyment) to a second instance – Pfaller gives the example of a man who, after he gave up drinking, became an excellent host by ensuring that his guests' glasses were constantly refilled[55] – it becomes immediately clear why the concept of interpassivity can be seen as a suitable analytical tool to grasp in its entirety why the history of human emancipation processes is also characterised by an unmistakable form of dialectic.

I explained this form of dialectic in one of my contributions for *Sublation Magazine*, using ChatGPT as an example. My thesis was, roughly speaking, that ChatGPT might one day ensure that we enter into a relationship of interpassivity with the chatbot, delegating the pleasure of interpreting and being critical of social problems to an AI system – the background assumption, of course, being that the critique of social problems generates pleasure. There can be, to put it briefly, no revolution and emancipation without a subject that enjoys. If human intelligence were to rely on a chatbot – whose interpretation is based on nothing more than probabilistic calculations – one would run the risk over time, to put it in line with Rosselli, that the principle of history would become an abstractum and that, as a consequence, human beings would not make history themselves, but rather be written by history. ChatGPT, to put it more polemically, is in this sense the historical materialism of the new digital-capitalist classes. A reliance on the ideology of digital emancipation will subsequently lead to emancipatory impotence and the concomitant extinction of the emancipatory subject.

Against the background of these considerations – and indeed I can definitely relate to this criticism – I could be accused of projecting relatively improbable and dystopian scenarios into the future and that I should rather deal with real social distortions instead of bourgeois sensitivities. I would like to counter this objection (or at least I will try to do so) with the following counter-objection: We are already in a post-emancipatory state.

The Delegation of Emancipatory Enjoyment in the Digital Sphere
Zygmunt Bauman once argued in his work *Socialism: The Active Utopia* what is lost when we delegate (as Rosselli once lamented)

our own responsibility for historical and social change to an abstraction called historical materialism. According to Bauman, the imagination of alternative utopian conceptions of society is to be regarded as a central ingredient for historical change, in that these "[...] pave the way for a critical attitude and a critical activity which alone can transform the present predicament of man".[56]

The critical and interactive confrontation with a deficient present requires, however, that human beings do not delegate their own creative capacity for critique and the accompanying imagination of alternative conceptions of society – which always presupposes a form of interactivity with the respective prevailing social conditions – to an AI system. The fact that forms of interpassivity already occur in other areas of the digital sphere has been abundantly and plausibly argued in various places.

Alfie Bown, for example, aptly points out that a form of interpassivity already manifests itself in the emoticon, which frees the user from the burden of a direct, i.e., interactive, emotion:

> When we react to a post with the laughing or shocked emoticon, for example, we are passing the obligation to react – and its associated pleasures – to the technology itself: we enjoy it interpassively, delegating pleasure to the machine so that we are not ourselves required to act. It's of course not that the 'react' emoticon is representative of the subject's real-life reaction (most people write 'lol' instead of laughing and not after laughing), so that we are clearly in the realm of interpassive pleasure with almost every online social engagement. If there is any truth in this suggestion, it at the very least shows the prevalence of interpassivity today.[57]

The emotional reaction that we as subjects are forced to express in everyday situations is thus delegated to an emoticon, which relieves us of the pressure to directly react. Moreover, this aspect draws attention to something else that has received rather little attention so far: The interpassive delegation of enjoyment – whether this relates to emotional reactions or to criticism of social injustice – opens up the space for completely new forms of hypocrisy. Even though one finds one's boss unsympathetic, one likes his or her profile picture in order to potentially gain that long-awaited promotion. Of course, even though this may seem like a banality at first, the whole thing becomes many times more interesting when the delegation of emancipatory pleasures to digital objects can be observed in the digital sphere. A good example of this can be seen in expressions of solidarity displayed as frames for profile pictures on Facebook. A symbol perceived as progressive is chosen – for example, the declarations of solidarity during the pandemic or, in the wake of the criminal war of aggression against Ukraine, the numerous Ukrainian flags – which appears on one's profile picture. At this point, however, it is not intended to discredit such expressions of solidarity (these can also have quite meaningful functions at other levels). Rather, it also becomes clear at this point that the emancipatory potential that arises from criticism of social grievances is delegated by the user to a digital function and he/she is thus relieved of the pressure to really act. However, the entire issue becomes even more problematic in this context when such contexts offer room for hypocrisy, since the respective emancipatory gesture expressed by the Facebook frame can also stand in glaring discrepancy (for whatever reason) to one's own actual attitude.

Interpassivity and the Post-Emancipatory Subject

Nevertheless, this problematic cannot be applied only to the realm of the digital sphere but seems to be of a more general character nowadays: We are rather dealing with a post-emancipatory subject. According to Van Oenen, the phenomenon of interpassivity can be seen as the post-emancipatory condition par excellence.[58]

The more human beings gain in emancipatory achievements, the more they develop – this is how I would like to put it at this point – a political superego, which constantly confronts them with the demand to live up to the emancipatory achievements and norms they have fought for. The previously won emancipatory achievements were made possible, as Van Oenen aptly points out, by the primacy of interactivity, which is specifically characterised by a critical confrontation with the empirical circumstances in order to subject these very empirical circumstances – for example, deficient social institutions – to lasting changes. The interactive critical confrontation with the respective circumstances must, however, always be characterised by the spirit of the utopian (to recur to Bauman) in the light of which the deficient social conditions are subjected to essential corrections (even if the utopia itself, according to its etymological origin, can never be achieved in fact). The interactively gained emancipatory achievements, however, produce an increasingly emancipatory individual who is no longer able to live up to these achievements:

> The privilege of self-realization embedded in the interactive condition virtually implies an imperative to self-realize, analogous to the "imperative to participate". Accordingly, individuals began to experience their emancipated, interactive status not only as a modern privilege, but more and more also as a burden. Interpassivity implies the shifting of this burden towards the entity with which one is – still – interactively connected: institutions in the case of society, artworks in the sphere of art. Thus we have effectively created a double shift: first we externalized our subjectivity to

institutions (or artworks), and now we also "outsource" the burden of interactivity and emancipation towards the institutions (or artworks).[59]

According to Van Oenen, however, it is not the case that the perceived burden of interactivity leads to a rejection of emancipatory ideals per se:

> It is important to see that outsourcing does not imply the rejection, or devaluation, of emancipatory ideals. On the contrary, it is precisely because we embrace these ideals, perhaps more than ever, that we feel unable to live up to them. We simply cannot self-realize in all aspects of life that have opened to us as modern, emancipated, and interactive beings. This is literally too much of a good thing for us. It is exactly because we want to be fully modern that we are increasingly unable to act consistently in accordance with our norms and ideals. [...] Naturally we feel ambiguous about this condition, because we do not readily admit that we fail to live up to our own norms and ideals. Perhaps we often do not even realize that this is the case; it is after all an unwelcome insight that the source of our discontent lies in failing to do what we ourselves consider the right thing to do.[60]

Here Van Oenen precisely draws attention to the dialectic of modern emancipation processes: While numerous struggles for emancipation – here Van Oenen mentions, for example, the revolts between 1965 and 1975, in which social institutions underwent substantial progressive changes – were characterised by the primacy of interactivity, in that the modern subject began to perceive itself as a historical entity and, as a consequence, to actively participate in the shaping of reality, the democratization of the public sphere was perceived as an increasing burden.

However, the modern interactive subject, whose actions have played an unmistakable influence in the creation of progressive social institutions, now finds itself confronted with a political superego that continually harasses it with demands to fully live up to the ethical standards it has achieved.

The post-emancipatory subject, on the other hand, seeks to delegate this burden (that is, not only its own subjectivity, but now also the interactive processes of emancipation) fully to social institutions.

Interpassivity Revisited: Letter to the Future AI

To close the line of argumentation (at least halfway) at this point, it is worth returning once again to the topic of artificial intelligence. The transhumanist Alexey Turchin has already illustrated the extent to which the increasing improvement of artificial intelligence contributes to us becoming a post-emancipatory subject. In a paper titled *Message to Any Future AI: "There are several instrumental reasons why exterminating humanity is not in your interest"*, Turchin explicitly addresses possible perfected future forms of AI with the request to deal with humanity as charitably as possible. Turchin's intention here is, of course, that his text will be read by a future AI.[61] Without going into too much detail here, however, one aspect is very striking: the request to (possible) future forms of AI to act according to honest moral principles and not to exterminate humanity brings the dialectic of modern processes of emancipation and the resulting interpassive (post-emancipatory) subject to the fore: even if AI has emerged from the creative mental capacities of human beings, at some point it begins to be superior to them, so that human beings become subservient to it. In other words: Humans begin to delegate not only their subjectivity – as is already the case in early stages of AI development – but also their interactivity and thus their emancipatory potential to not even existing forms of future AI by admitting their own powerlessness (instead of stopping such development processes here and now). Similarly, as Rosselli already argued at back then – even if historical materialism is a helpful instrument for the analysis of social development processes! – that the sole belief in historical materialism has put the Italian workers' movement into a form of incapacity to act, it is in this context the delegation of one's own capacity to act to AI.

What to Do? The Bite from the Apple and the Condemnation from Paradise

Erich Fromm has already pointed out in all clarity that Adam and Eve's fall into sin is to be regarded retrospectively as inevitable and as the most radical act of human freedom.[62] In a similar way as the foetus in the womb – this concretely characterises the existential dichotomy of human existence according to Fromm – Adam and Eve still live in complete harmony with nature in the Garden of Eden but have not yet transcended it in the light of their own freedom. The disobedience accompanying the bite into the apple and the consequent damnation from paradise (similar to the biological detachment from the mother produced by the severing of the umbilical cord) is thus, according to Fromm's reading, characterised by a radical form of inevitability. Only condemnation subsequently leads to becoming human and to an awareness of oneself and the concomitant possibility of acting as a historical subject capable of action. Fromm's metaphor seems to provide an extremely helpful (if not definitive) response to the paradox of the post-emancipatory subject: Unity with the Garden of Eden – the mother's umbilical cord – cannot be restored, and we are ruthlessly at the mercy of this impotence. Instead of delegating the responsibility resulting from this sin to instances that (supposedly) carry out our interactivity, we should repeat the act of sin again and again and risk damnation from paradise. In other words: to separate ourselves from what is suggested as possible and to dare the sinful act of the impossible. This can only be done through active voluntarism and the constantly recurring confrontation with what exists. Neither an AI nor historical development trends can take this responsibility from us.

7

Further Reflections on Interpassivity, or the Outsourced Revolution

At the beginning of 2022, Jürgen Habermas caused a debate with an article in the *Süddeutsche Zeitung* (a famous German newspaper) that not only polarised German society in a considerable way. In this essay, titled *War and Outrage*, Habermas warns urgently against a military escalation of the war of aggression waged by Russia against Ukraine. The interesting thing that emerges from a closer analysis of Habermas's essay, however, is that the primary criticism that Habermas makes is not directed at German political decision-makers. Rather, Habermas is in favour of German Chancellor Olaf Scholz's hesitant stance with regard to the delivery of further military equipment to Ukraine (often contemptuously labelled as "hesitation and procrastination" in the German media). Habermas's criticism is rather directed at the general social discourse itself. The outrage that Habermas's essay provoked in many parts of the population can primarily be explained by the fact that they were able to read something into Habermas's essay that Habermas did not want to express in the slightest (which in turn is a clear indication that those who joined in the chorus of outrage with regard to Habermas's essay have not read Habermas's essay): Habermas, by arguing that the West must be careful not to let the conflict escalate and bring the world closer to the danger of nuclear escalation, would force Ukraine into submission. However, nothing could be further from Habermas's actual argument, which is why it seems worthwhile at this point to cite Habermas in more detail:

In view of the risk of world conflagration, which must be avoided at all costs, the uncertainty of this decision leaves no room for risky poker. Even if the West were cynical enough to take the "warning" of one of these "small" nuclear weapons into account as a risk, i.e. to accept it at worst, who could guarantee that the escalation could still be stopped? What remains is a scope for arguments that must be carefully weighed up in the light of the necessary technical knowledge and all the necessary information, which is not always publicly available, in order to be able to make well-founded decisions. The West, which has left no doubt about its de facto involvement in the war by imposing drastic sanctions from the outset, must therefore carefully weigh up every further step of military support to see whether it is crossing the indeterminate line of formal entry into the war, which depends on Putin's power of definition.[63]

First of all, Habermas draws attention to something that should be a commonplace in normative terms: In the face of the nuclear risk posed by the war in Ukraine, Putin's threats must be taken quite seriously – even, and this is the crux of the matter, if one assumes that Putin only wants to intimidate the West. Habermas addresses a very pertinent point with this form of argumentation. What many of those representatives who argue that Putin's constant threats are nothing more than intimidation fail to recognise is a crucial aspect: *the role of ignorance*. It is worth comparing this with the lines of argumentation that have repeatedly emerged at a social and discursive level during the coronavirus pandemic. Most of the measures that were enacted – at least in my home country of Germany – during the coronavirus pandemic and (optionally) weakened again, also had to constantly refer to the fact of *not knowing* as the most basic point of legitimacy. The lack of epistemic availability regarding the potential danger of the virus (due to a lack of scientific knowledge) rightly called for tougher intervention by political decision-makers at the beginning of the pandemic. Those politically initiated measures – such as curfews or the wearing of face masks – were primarily aimed at protecting members of society from the danger of the Covid-19 virus. However, as scientific knowledge of the nature and potential danger of the virus increased, the corresponding measures were constantly adapted and adjusted. Those who take the position regarding the war in Ukraine that Putin merely wants to intimidate the West with his constant threats are making a dangerous mistake: the trial-and-error approach that characterised the coronavirus pandemic is being applied, even if not consciously intended, to the war in Ukraine. This can be illustrated particularly well by past media discourses in my home country, Germany. At the beginning of the war in Ukraine, for example, there was a largely prevailing consensus that no heavy military weapons should be sent to Ukraine – a decision which, as reality shows, has recently been revised and is no longer accessible to a broad social discourse. A similar pattern can be observed with regard to the discourse surrounding the Leopard tank. Initially, there was a broad consensus that the delivery of such a tank could lead to an inevitable escalation. However, as the pressure on German Chancellor Scholz increased, this taboo was finally discarded and the tank was delivered.[64] Now, at the beginning of 2024, it remains a matter of time before Chancellor Scholz abandons his reluctance to deliver Taurus cruise missiles – which, according to experts, could cause a not inconsiderable potential for escalation.[65] What the previous statements are primarily intended to illustrate is the fact that an approach based on trial and error (which may seem entirely plausible in a pandemic) harbours an immediate potential for escalation, as an error (in the form of a nuclear escalation) may occur under certain circumstances, making a new attempt impossible.

When Habermas argues that the sheer danger of such a world conflagration leaves no room for risky poker, he is pointing out precisely this fact: against the backdrop of epistemic uncertainties, an experimental approach – in the form of tests to determine whether a further supply of weapons will lead to an escalation of war – can lead to a further error negating such an approach itself. Or, to put it differently: A certain form of negation takes place, which does not lead to negation of negation (and thus to a better world), but to the end of the existing world in the first place:

> The argument that Putin should not be backed into a corner because he would then be capable of anything is therefore countered by the argument that it is only this "policy of fear" that gives the opponent a free hand to drive forward the escalation of the conflict step by step [...]. Of course, this argument also only confirms the character of a situation that is difficult to predict. For as long as we are determined for good reasons not to enter the war as another party for the protection of Ukraine, the type and scope of military support must also be qualified from this point of view. Anyone who opposes a "policy of fear" in a rationally justifiable way is already within the scope of argumentation of the politically responsible and factually well-informed consideration that Chancellor Olaf Scholz rightly insists on.[66]

It is important to note that Habermas affirms that military support for Ukraine is not only morally, but also strategically necessary – which reduces the accusations against Habermas that he is arguing for the subjugation of Ukraine out of concern to absurdity. Reading between Habermas's lines, it is particularly interesting to note that it is indeed extremely important to oppose a policy based entirely on fear (an accusation that is often made against the pacifist position). However, Habermas reinforces this statement with the very important addition that the advocacy against a "politics of fear" must be carried out in a rationally justifiable way – here one is naturally inclined to recognise a link to Habermas's discourse ethics. But what would such a rationally justifiable approach look like in this context? One could argue that recognizing the *non-knowledge* of the situation apostrophised above would be an important first step.

In the further course of his argumentation, however, Habermas draws attention to another important aspect that deserves attention in this context: a victory in Ukraine, according to Habermas, is a dangerous illusion of the West, which ultimately claims more and more Ukrainian lives – according to Habermas, this seems to be a morally precarious starting position, especially because the West is sitting in a kind of spectator's box:

> But isn't it pious self-deception to bet on a Ukrainian victory against the murderous Russian warfare without taking up arms yourself? The warmongering rhetoric does not sit well with the spectator box from which it eloquently emanates. After all, it does not invalidate the unpredictability of an opponent who could put all his eggs in one basket.[67]

It may be argued that Pistorius's recent remarks on the subject of "readiness for war" cast legitimate doubt on the thesis that the West can never get into the dangerous situation of being drawn into this war.

Nevertheless, Habermas's statement that the West is observing the whole event from a spectator's box and, in a second step, trying to make normative judgements about whether Ukraine can win or not based on these observations is interesting. One could almost be inclined (to venture a recourse to previous arguments) to understand this spectator box of the West on a symbolic level as a form of patriotic interpassivity. For the average political observer in the West, Ukraine thus symbolises the patriotic subject that can live out the excessive inclination to patriotism suppressed in the West through affect regulation. At this point, however, the dark flip side of such logic inevitably becomes clear: this patriotic subject does not exist – on the contrary, more and more people are losing their lives in Ukraine every day. Now, at the beginning of 2024, when these lines are being written, it seems that Ukraine will indeed lose the war and that the opportunities for constructive negotiations have long since passed.[68]

However, this form of interpassive delegation of one's own (unconscious) needs also shows itself in other aspects of the war in Ukraine. This also became clear last year during Prigozhin's uprising against the Kremlin. Those who can still remember that situation will notice the euphoria that prevailed in the West about the fact that nothing less than a revolution was taking place in Russia – without realising what kind of person Prigozhin was. Benjamin Studebaker has recently made this point in an extremely apt analysis, pointing out that Prigozhin brought about that (albeit unconscious) desire for revolution that seems to be increasingly disappearing in Western society – thus Studebaker points out (in the spirit of revolutionary interpassivity) that Prigozhin offered a form of over-identification for the Western online user that dares not to dream of a possible improvement in liberal-capitalist social relations:

The online westerner could identify with this revolutionary figure without themselves having to do anything revolutionary. Safe behind the screen, the revolution could be watched and enjoyed without any of its attendant dangers. Unlike say, January 6th, the westerner was free to support this rebellion without incurring any moral censure. For the liberal centrist, nationalism is forbidden – unless it is nationalism on behalf of Ukraine. In the same way, revolution is an assault on all the institutions we are meant to hold dear – unless it is committed in Russia against Putin. When discussing Ukraine – and only when discussing Ukraine – the liberal subject is free from the straightjacket of having to be a liberal, able to endorse all of the things that in any other context cannot be tolerated.[69]

According to Studebaker, the liberal subject – or the average Western online user – is characterised by the fact that their own liberal worldview can only be maintained by a dark flip side. The maintenance of one's own liberal attitude – as Studebaker's explanations more than clairvoyantly point out – can only be guaranteed by the interpassive delegation of one's own revolutionary longing to a non-liberal subject. Here, too, it becomes clear that the liberal subject always finds itself in a field of tension between its political *superego* and its political *id* (which secretly longs for change towards a better world). However, Studebaker deepens this idea in an interesting way by pointing out that this revolutionary desire itself reflects the perceived lack of alternatives in the liberal-capitalist economic system:

Deep down, the online westerner pines for revolution in Russia in part because we no longer believe in our own system. Yet, at the same time, we cannot imagine another political system that would be worth dying for. Our faith in the capacity of human beings to build better societies has been ground down by the experience of failed revolutions. So, a revolution in Russia gives us what we want in a double sense – it allows us to have the revolution we can no longer have for ourselves, and it reinforces the sense that the western system is inevitable, that all other systems eventually succumb to it. If our system is inevitable, it doesn't matter how many legitimate criticisms we may have of it – we have to tolerate it. Any alternative we might cook up must immediately be likened to the phantoms of the past – the Soviet Union or the Third Reich – and thrown into the trash can of history. But we are allowed to enjoy the fall of alternative political systems, to enjoy the process of political and economic homogenization as it unfolds.[70]

The – initially unconscious – declining belief in an alternative to their own system prompts the liberal subject to seek out this change elsewhere (or at least the possibility of change). The interpassive gesture is unmistakably clear here: the (potential) pleasure that a revolution could bring is delegated by the liberal subject to an actor who takes over the revolution for the liberal subject. The political superego ensures that the liberal subject adopts Thatcher's dictum of no alternatives and develops feelings of guilt if it even thinks a revolutionary thought that relates to the Western liberal-capitalist economic system. At the same time, this political superego is not able to completely eliminate the desire for revolution – the urge for change seems unavoidable; all the more so against the backdrop of the multiple crises we are confronted with today. Taking action into our own hands (and not hoping for a revolution of a type like Prigozhin) would be a first step in the right direction.

8

The Regressive Illusions of Jordan Peterson, or About a Postmodern Drinking Song[5]

A phenomenon that has been largely underrepresented in media coverage (at least until now) is the Postmodernist Drinking Song[71] published by Canadian psychologist Jordan B. Peterson. In the video, Peterson plays a food delivery man – with a cap showing the inscription Taco Gulag – who arrives at his flat after work and switches on the television. An analysis of the music video indicates that the food delivery man played by Peterson is a left-wing activist – i.e. a member of the group of social movements that Peterson repeatedly subjects to vehement criticism. In the course of the music video, the food delivery man played by Peterson sings to a song on his television set, in which various intellectual theorists of postmodern thought (such as Jacques Derrida, Michel Foucault or Judith Butler) appear.

The lyrics of the song make it all even more apparent that Peterson has finally left the metier of the traditional conservative characterised by decency and manners in the form of his criticism.

It cannot be the aim of this essay to go into these unspeakable lines. Just this much: what Peterson seems to be attempting here is an ironic appropriation of supposedly postmodern ways of argumentation from the conservative side. Peterson's attempt can, of course, only be understood through the background assumption that today's forms of left-wing identity politics and cancel culture are characterised by a particularly high degree

---

5   This article was previously published by *Sublation Magazine*. Slight reformulations have been made.

of aggressiveness, in that dissenting opinions are aggressively suppressed or even cancelled. Peterson attempts to make such aggressive forms of discourse his own by – and here lies the seemingly consciously intended paradox in Peterson's video – singing against postmodern and post-structuralist thinkers from the perspective of a progressive activist (which of course raises the question of coherence/logic: How can it be that a progressive activist sings such anti progressive content?).

It is particularly striking that the flat of the activist played by Peterson seems untidy, which is why the viewer is easily prompted at this point to make a connection to Peterson's famous dictum "Set your house in order!".[72] In addition, the activist's room is characterised by an extremely childish-looking lamp – possibly a reference to Peterson's view that most activists should be regarded as infantile rather than adults. Although the video may seem absurd, it is unsurprising when one considers Peterson's thinking as a whole.

Jordan Peterson, who previously taught at the University of Toronto and is a member of the *intellectual dark web* alongside thinkers such as Ben Shapiro and Dave Rubin, basically continues the criticism in the song that has made him stand out and intervene in public debates in recent years: The video clearly expresses the contempt that Peterson and his fan community have for postmodern and post-structuralist theorising, which – according to Peterson's argument – does not allow for a clear interpretation of the question of how the world is to be perceived.[73] Or to put it another way: There is no objective truth and, therefore, no morally impeccable ideological worldview. However, Peterson's criticism is not directed against postmodern and post-structuralist thinking per se, but against the (allegedly existing) group that Peterson calls *postmodern Marxists*.[74] With regard to a possible compatibility between postmodern thinking and Marxist theorising, Peterson expresses himself as follows:

It's not as if I personally think that postmodernism and Marxism are commensurate. It's obvious to me that the much-vaunted "scepticism towards grand narratives" that is part and parcel of the postmodern viewpoint makes any such alliance logically impossible. Postmodernists should be as sceptical towards Marxism as towards any other canonical belief system. So the formal postmodern claim, such as it is, is radical scepticism. But that's not at all how it has played out in theory or in practice. Derrida and Foucault were, for example, barely repentant Marxists, if repentant at all. They parleyed their 1960's bourgeoisie vs proletariat rhetoric into the identity politics that has plagued us since the 1970's [sic]. Foucault's fundamental implicit (and often explicit) claim is that power relations govern society. That's a rehashing of the Marxist claim of eternal and primary class warfare. Derrida's hypothetical concern for the marginalised is a version of the same thing. I don't really care if either of them made the odd statement about disagreeing with the Marxist doctrines: their fundamental claims are still soaked in those patterns of thought.[75]

If one reads between the lines, it first becomes unmistakably clear that Peterson is trying to dispel a point of criticism frequently levelled by his left-wing critics. This point of criticism is based on the quite correct thesis that the concept of postmodern Marxism is basically nothing more than an oxymoron. In this context, Luke Savage draws attention in a clear-sighted analysis to the fact that a central distinguishing feature between postmodern/ poststructuralist thinking and Marxist theory formation lies precisely in the fact that *Marxism is an inherently structuralist theory*, while poststructuralism is associated with a fundamental scepticism towards socio-political utopias and narratives of progress.[76] Savage goes on to write that "(i)n stark contrast to Marxism, both postmodernism and poststructuralism are closely associated with scepticism toward historical master narratives and doubt about the possibility (and desirability) of deep foundations in politics, metaphysics, epistemology, and literary criticism"[77]. The scepticism implicit in poststructuralist thinking thus to a certain extent cancels out the claim, contained in Marxism, to a scientific analysis of the material structural relations of capitalist social orders. Now back to Peterson's statement: on a theoretical level, Peterson seems to confirm the objection raised by critics such as Savage. The scepticism towards grand narratives present in postmodern thinking does not seem to be compatible with traditional Marxist thinking from Peterson's point of view either.[78]

In the further course of his argument, however, Peterson draws attention to the fact that there seems to be a glaring contradiction – and according to Peterson's reading, the basic theoretical assumption of postmodern Marxism seems to be based on this contradiction – between postmodern (formal) theory formation and postmodern practice.[79] If postmodernists also felt committed to their basic theoretical premises in their practical actions, according to Peterson's thesis, they should "[...] be as sceptical towards Marxism as towards any other canonical belief system".[80]

According to Peterson, this fundamental scepticism is not adhered to in the slightest by postmodern theorists when it comes to their socio-political commitment. Referring in particular to Foucault, Peterson draws attention to the extent to which a (supposedly) Marxist basic premise characterises the practice of postmodern thought: The ubiquitous presence of power structures. Against the background of the assumption that a large part of socio-political upheavals can be explained by the omnipresence of power relations, the narrative of the struggle between the bourgeoisie and the proletariat, which was still predominant in the 1960s, was transformed into the narrative of a struggle for the recognition of different identities (today commonly known as identity politics).[81]

According to Peterson, Derrida also helped shape these fundamental theoretical considerations. Therefore, it is initially irrelevant for Peterson whether theorists such as Foucault or Derrida publicly postulate that they disagree with many of the basic premises of Marxist theorising. Ultimately, the common ground between postmodern and Marxist theorists lies precisely in the fact that social structural relations are determined by power. In Marxist theorising, this fact is reflected in the assumption that class struggles – and thus also struggles against the power of capital – are characteristic of societies and their developmental tendencies.[82] According to Peterson's interpretation, the struggle for recognition emanating from the marginalised, as is characteristic of identity politics, is based on the same premise. This (alleged) commonality subsequently characterises the enemy image of postmodern Marxists proclaimed by Peterson and his followers.

Against the background of the above considerations, one might be inclined to ask what problem Peterson has with the postmodernists' assumption that they feel compelled to critically analyse power relations. In the further course of his argument, Peterson draws attention to the fact that postmodern theorists have no ethics whatsoever in their practical actions (whatever Peterson means by this in concrete terms, this concept is not spelt out in more detail, at least in Peterson's argument cited here). Furthermore, Peterson laments that the actions of postmodern theorists are not characterised by a particularly high degree of coherence, however, and this is where the most obvious paradox in Peterson's argumentation comes to light, Peterson's way of arguing is not characterised by a particularly high degree of coherence either:

> Postmodernism leaves its practitioners without an ethic. Action in the world (even perception) is impossible without an ethic, so one has to be at least allowed in through the back door. The fact that such allowance produces a logical contradiction appears to bother the low-rent postmodernists who dominate the social sciences and humanities not at all. Then again, coherence isn't one of their strong points (and the demand for such coherence can just be read as another patriarchal imposition typifying oppressive Western thought).[83]

What is impressive about the passage quoted here is that it is actually empty of content. And what does Peterson mean by ethics? Isn't it a major achievement of the Enlightenment to question certain narratives and authorities?

It is by no means my intention at this point to defend postmodern theorising and modern practices of identity politics – these theoretical currents and political movements can certainly be subjected to justified points of criticism, but these must be based on an accurate analysis. Luke Savage, for example, more than aptly points out that many of today's identity politics struggles are problematic precisely because they often lack a materialist analysis of social development trends (which then results in the fact that large corporations such as Amazon are committed to identity politics issues, but leave class and power relations largely untouched):

> Plenty of mainstream social justice critiques today, after all, quite visibly lack a class or materialist dimension and, in some cases, can be embraced by powerful institutions for that very reason. Corporate behemoths like Amazon are all too keen to adopt the regalia of social justice, but they're definitely not trying to eliminate social

hierarchy or create a classless society. In much the same way, plenty of centrist and liberal politicians who might endorse the broad idea of "intersectionality" would be loath to advocate anything beyond the most incremental and market-based reforms (and, in many cases, are deeply hostile to transformative policymaking of any kind). [...] (M)uch of mainstream social justice politics today is quite specifically defined by its aversion to the totalising theories and holistic explanations associated with modernism: emphasising instead the dynamics of interpersonal relations, the mechanics of language, and the recognition of particular identities. There's nothing necessarily wrong with any of these things, of course, but they hardly belong to an all-encompassing or utopian project.[84]

Many of today's social movements, which are often characterised by post-structuralist and postmodern forms of theorising, focus too much on the particular – in the form of sexual, ethnic or other characteristics – and not on the *universal*, as Savage rightly points out. In other words: Even if the intentions of many of the social movements can certainly be seen as honest, they fail to recognise a crucial point: instead of focusing on politically correct forms of expression or on unintentional and subtle forms of discrimination, it would make far more sense to look again at the socio-economic distortions. The *universal* would therefore be, in Savage's words, a utopian project that would resolve these particular problems itself. But Peterson and his followers do not want to see this universalistic stance. Instead, they persist in their particularistic attitude and pursue a right-wing form of identity politics themselves.

9

Solidarity and Its Contradictions

Whether it is the struggle of the labour movement, the advocacy of freedom rights or intra-familial relationships (of course, countless other examples can be cited): The principle of interpersonal solidarity is not only formative, but also necessary for the smooth functioning of social coexistence. This can also extend to fundamental areas of interpersonal life that often transform human existence, such as love. In *Man for Himself*, for example, Erich Fromm[85] clairvoyantly points out that love is to be regarded as a fundamental ability that does not initially differentiate between the self and the other. In other words: According to Fromm, there is a fundamental difference (already evident in scholastic philosophy)[86] between a narcissistic personality disposition and the principle of self-love. While the former, according to Fromm, is to be classified as a clear form of pathology, the latter represents the basic condition for the ability to love at all. Fromm sums up this idea in *Man for Himself* as follows:

> Not only others, but we ourselves are the "object" of our feelings and attitudes; the attitudes toward others and toward ourselves, far from being contradictory, are basically conjunctive. With regard to the problem under discussion this means: Love of others and love of ourselves are not alternatives. On the contrary, an attitude of love toward themselves will be found in all those who are capable of loving others. Love, in principle, is indivisible as far as the connection between "objects" and one's own self is concerned.[87]

According to Fromm, love for oneself and one's nearest and dearest (the child, the partner, the parents, etc.) are not a contradiction, but the basic condition for love in general. According to Fromm, love thus represents something radically indivisible, which eludes all forms of alternative interpretation schemes.

Hegel also starts from the idea that love presupposes a difference – there is me and the other – but at the same time negates this difference and thus turns it into a paradox, which is itself constitutive of the essence of love. This becomes particularly clear[88] when Hegel points out that love means that *one can be with oneself in the other*. Todd McGowan expresses Hegel's thought as follows:

> Love fascinates the young Hegel because it represents the identification of contraries and the sustaining of contradiction as a positive force. When one is in love, one unites one's own identity with that of the other. The lover and the beloved become one in their way of finding satisfaction. Lovers do not just privilege the other's satisfaction over their own but adopt the other's satisfaction as their own. And yet love would not be love if a distinction between subject and beloved other did not remain. The act of love requires at once the elimination of difference and its perpetuation.[89]

McGowan expresses the essence of Hegelian contradiction here in an incomparable way. At first, one might assume that (the young) Hegel starts from the pathos of becoming one that is typical of subjects in love – the loving subject subsequently derives its own satisfaction from the satisfaction of the other. Here, of course, the possibly gloomy flip side of the loving (and thus solidarity-practising) subject becomes clear. What if the other person – according to the Hegelian definition – is not loving and their own satisfaction is constituted by the fact that the other subject is truly loving? To put it more concretely: as soon as only one of the two subjects in a love relationship feels a true form of love (and expresses their own love by practising it on the basis of these feelings), the lover is put into a subjugated position. However, as McGowan also aptly points out, Hegel cleverly overcomes this (possible) objection on an argumentative level by pointing out that, despite the potential for becoming one, there is still difference. Despite the necessity of the abolition of difference (the loving subjects each make the happiness of the other their own), this very difference must continue to exist simultaneously (if the subject can only be with itself in the other, the subject must still exist as a disparate self as a consequence). In a sense, one could add Hegel's thoughts to those of Fromm: Self-love is not to be equated with a form of narcissism precisely for the reason that the happiness of the other person is also perceived as being one's own in each case. But what happens, as already indicated, if the abolition of that difference from which love relationships can be constituted in the first place does not take place at all in one of the two loving subjects?

Here it is worth leaving the thematic field of pure love relationships and looking at the flip side that can form the basis of solidary relationships – be they of a partnership, family or socio-political nature (class struggle is also based on the principle of solidarity): the ability to empathise with others.

The cognitive scientist Fritz Breithaupt[90] recently wrote in his book *The Dark Sides of Empathy* that on a cultural level, the false analogy is all too often drawn between the ability to empathise and moral action. It is true that the ability to empathise can help people to intensify their own feelings and expand the spectrum of perceptions. Nevertheless, according to Breithaupt, there is not necessarily a close connection between morality and empathy. In this context, Breithaupt emphasises:

To begin with the question of morality, empathy can be used for both good and bad ends. As we have seen, an empathetic torturer is plausible [...]. Empathy can, of course, motivate positive, prosocial actions. There is a parent's primal empathetic connection to their child. (I do not question that this form of empathy may have been a driving force of the evolution of empathy in mammals, and in humans in particular [...]). Even parental concerns are not so straightforward, though. Helicopter parents, after all, want what's best for their children, though they may mistake that impulse with more selfish ends. People can also empathize for the sake of feeling empathy or in order to gain access to the feelings of another person, not to help or support them. In these cases, empathy becomes self-serving, independent of moral considerations.[91]

In this context, Breithaupt clairvoyantly points out that the capacity for empathy can be both morally good and questionable in terms of its purpose. For example, a person who intends to torture another person may have an extremely pronounced capacity for empathy (only if one is aware of the physical and psychological weaknesses can one inflict harm on this person in the most effective way possible). According to Breithaupt, the situation is similar with the phenomenon of helicopter parents: even if the natural care of one's own offspring is not only understandable from an evolutionary biology point of view, but also represents a moral necessity, altruistic and genuinely selfish objectives can easily be confused with one another, especially in the phenomenon of overprotection.

Even apart from these examples, further examples can be cited: A relationship (at other historical periods) between a slave and his slave master can also be characterised by empathy in extreme cases, in that the subjugated person always internalises the will of the subjugator as his own. The same could be understood with regard to abusive forms of loving relationships – to refer back to what was mentioned at the beginning: The victim may develop empathy for the partner out of compassion and subsequently tries to sympathise with the partner's (physical or mental) acts of violence (and in extreme cases blames him-/herself and perceives these acts as an actual form of legitimate punishment). A similar approach can be taken with regard to autocratic leaders, in that their ideologies are internalised so vehemently that they appear to be the only coherent world view.

Now, to return to Fromm, the fact of empathy is in a certain way unavoidable. Only in the presence of our social integration do we constitute ourselves as true subjects. This also becomes clear with the Marxist-influenced proletarian subject: one's own position in the production process (and thus one's own alienation) can only be abolished if one comes to the realisation that one's own situation of alienation is to be understood as a phenomenon that unites all proletarian subjects.

According to Fromm,[92] a central characteristic of human life is that it represents a transcendence of the natural conditions of existence, but at the same time is to be regarded as a part of these very conditions. In other words: in contrast to animals, humans have a much higher degree of cognitive (and a lower degree of instinctive) endowment. At the same time, however, man's more highly developed cognitive capacities mean that he develops an awareness of himself and the loneliness of his own existence (in light of the realisation that man can never fully return to the natural realm). Due to this circumstance, man tries to establish various forms of relationships with the outside world – which, according to Fromm's interpretation, can be both productive and destructive in nature.

If one wants to understand bonds of solidarity as something positive, it is essential to shed light on their dark sides. In the end, Marx's famous dictum from the Communist Manifesto can also be referred to. When Marx points out towards the end of the second chapter that communism is characterised precisely by the fact that "[...] the free development of each is the condition for the free development of all",[93] Marx is simultaneously hinting at the fact – if one is willing to analyse Marx's statement in the light of the aforementioned elaborations – that true solidarity is only possible if the proletarian subject is also able to establish this solidarity with itself. Formulated somewhat more polemically: There is no revolution without self-love.

10

How to Think in the Face of Crisis?

There is no shortage of catastrophes (that much can be said at this point) at the start of 2024: The conflict in the Middle East, the war in Ukraine, the climate crisis and an increasing shift to the political right in many countries around the world – not to mention other crises. In fact, the situation currently seems so catastrophic for many people (I can confirm this from personal experience) that some found it difficult to wish everyone a Happy New Year. One is almost inclined to return to the role of philosophy as apostrophised by Adorno in *Minima Moralia*: In view of the catastrophes facing humanity in 2024, a philosophy that is still justifiable in times of despair is "[...] the attempt to view all things as they would present themselves from the standpoint of redemption."[94]

Here, Adorno should indeed be read with the precision that his quote deserves. First, Adorno abandons an idea that one is most inclined to think regarding catastrophic development processes, i.e. that in view of the nature of the crisis, it is more than naïve to even mentally practise any form of hope. According to Adorno, however, the exact opposite is the case: precisely the impossibility of realising a utopian point of refuge within social conditions should lead us to regard this as the only legitimate position that a philosopher can take in order to free him-/herself from his/her bias within the social totality – and consequently, on a conceptual level, to emancipate him-/herself from this very totality.[95]

What Adorno expresses in this passage of *Minima Moralia* can easily be applied to the dictum put forward by Marx (already mentioned in the previous chapters) which he expresses in his introduction to the *Critique of Hegel's Philosophy of Right*.

The social totality is also dependent on the illusion of all the actors involved in it for its own reproduction – to go beyond this totality (or to transcend it) thus seems to resemble an act of impossibility: The standpoint of redemption can ultimately only lead to a state in which the social totality – together with all the illusions that are necessary to maintain it – itself undergoes a negation. The question that subsequently arises with regard to the current situation is: Is there still a point of view of redemption (understood as a utopian point of view) that exists outside of the existing social coordinates? Or, as one could also assume, is this standpoint, in the best utopian sense, a *non-place* that is inconceivable within the social totality?

Even if this may sound pessimistic at first, it does indeed seem impossible to look at things from the perspective of redemption – as a result, there can indeed be, to put it again with Adorno, no right life in the wrong one. However, there is an additional remark to be made here: Becoming aware with regard to one's own entanglement in the totality of social conditions can lead to becoming aware of this involvement in the "wrong life". Becoming aware of those regressive illusions (which are necessary for the maintenance of social totality) is by no means a foregone conclusion.

The Middle East Conflict and the Question of Mourning
The Middle East conflict, which has been reignited since October 7, also raises the question of how the current world situation can best be viewed from the standpoint of redemption. Here, too, it is clear – especially in my home country of Germany – that the fronts are more than hardened. For example, especially after the cruel attack on Israel by Hamas, the German debate (for historically understandable reasons) took the view that we must now unconditionally stand by Israel. There were also warnings of an increasing rise in anti-Semitism. What is really worrying, however, is not only the fact that this fight against

anti-Semitism is also being exploited by right-wing parties in Germany to place the population of Arab origin living here under general suspicion. Furthermore, it seems that standing up for the interests of innocent Palestinian civilians and the fight against anti-Semitism are dismissed as a contradiction. In other words: It is assumed that one must now unconditionally support the Israeli government – if one does not do so, one does not subsequently declare war on anti-Semitism in a truly convincing way. This also shows the extent to which the German debate is based on an extremely dangerous form of regressive illusion: The regressive illusion of tribalism, which can also be found in (both right-wing and left-wing) forms of identity politics. What this argumentative logic negates, however, is the universal, which includes victims on both the Israeli and Palestinian sides. Tribalist logic assumes that there is only one particular point of view, which consequently leads to the reprehensible view that the Middle East conflict is a form of antagonism in which – from a moral point of view – only one side can be supported. Particularly in left-wing and post-colonial circles, this leads to the ideologically blinded assumption that Hamas is waging a liberation struggle against a colonial regime. But the other side does not really have any more convincing arguments to offer either: The bombing of the Gaza Strip and all the civilians killed in the process are, after all, a necessary evil that must be accepted without ifs and buts. It is even worse in the German discourse: the fight against anti-Semitism takes on a new form of disguised racism, in which the entire Muslim and Arab population is subjected to general suspicion. This has been expressed more than aptly by the American-German writer and secular Jew Deborah Feldman. According to Feldman, the only lesson to be learned from the Holocaust (and Feldman makes this clear with reference to Holocaust survivors such as the authors Primo Levi, Jean Améry and Jorge Semprún) is the unconditional defence of human rights in general.[96] In other words: the unconditional defence of universalism, which abstracts from characteristics such as gender or origin – in the sense of a radical postulate of equality – and places being human itself in the foreground. Judith Butler illustrates this universal standpoint from which the situation with regard to the Middle East conflict must be analysed in an incomparable way using the example of mourning. According to Butler, the ability to mourn should refer to both the victims of the Israeli and the victims of the Palestinian side – without, Butler makes this important addition, getting bogged down in debates about relativism or equivalence:

> I ask myself whether we can mourn, without qualification, for the lives lost in Israel as well as those lost in Gaza without getting bogged down in debates about relativism and equivalence. Perhaps the wider compass of mourning serves a more substantial ideal of equality, one that acknowledges the equal grievability of lives, and gives rise to an outrage that these lives should not have been lost, that the dead deserved more life and equal recognition for their lives.[97]

The compass of mourning – as Butler's elaborations impressively point out – is in its natural state oriented towards a more substantial ideal of human equality. Mourning (as an emotional dimension and a fact of human existence) is able to transcend particular standpoints and the resulting antagonisms arising from political-theoretical considerations. The mourning for the people in Gaza and the mourning for the victims of the attack carried out by Hamas on October 7 does not represent a contradiction, but points in the direction of the only true standpoint of redemption, as it was once apostrophised by Adorno in *Minima Moralia*.

Epilogue

On the Necessity of Illusions, or the Return of the Repressed

When talking about regressive illusions, it is important to focus attention solely on the adjective *regressive* – and not to assume, as one might intuitively be inclined to do at first, that illusions are to be classified as something thoroughly bad that makes the search for a more profound truth impossible. The German journalist Titus Blome points out that a certain degree of self-deception can be helpful from time to time (in contrast to the frequently cited assumption that there is an individual unconscious that must inevitably be brought to consciousness):

> Of course you are now saying that self-deception is unrealistic wishful thinking. True, but you're forgetting in how many situations in life unrealistic wishful thinking is the best solution. With enough affirmative self-hypnosis, you can sometimes simply talk yourself into having the self-confidence to make it big in life: Of course you're good enough for this job or that artistic risk. The basis for this? I made it up, thank you very much.[98]

In the light of these lines, one could easily be led to believe that Marx's aforementioned dictum – that the demand to abandon illusions about one's own (social, socio-economic, etc.) condition is tantamount to the demand to abandon a condition whose stability/reproduction is dependent on our own illusions – is clearly refuted here. Self-deception in the form of an illusion regarding one's own social situation can be helpful from time to time. But how does this idea fit in with those of Marx in his introduction to the *Critique of Hegel's Philosophy of Right*? First of

73

all, it is helpful to point out that the illusionary self-deception Marx is talking about relates to his famous critique of religion according to whose basic thesis religion is an opium *of the* people. In other words: Religious belief is to be seen as a form of regressive illusion, which serves to conceal one's own entanglement in the social totality and subsequently makes socio-political change impossible. Here it is worth citing Marx himself:

> Religious misery is in one sense the expression of real misery and in another the protest against real misery. Religion is the sigh of the oppressed creature, the spirit of a heartless world, as it is the spirit of spiritless conditions.[99]

Here it becomes clear why the concept of religion coined by Marx, with regard to the criteria that characterise it, serves as a paradigmatic example of the phenomenon subsumed under the term *regressive illusion* in this book. Regressive illusions – even if they do not necessarily refer to religious forms of interpreting the world – always imply a dialectic between expression and rebellion, or as in Marx: between expression and protest. This can be illustrated using various examples, some of which were also discussed in the previous chapters. The typical Trump or AfD voter (or far-right voters in general) expresses their own social situation (which is often characterised by a considerable degree of misery/socio-economic disadvantage) through their own ideological stance. But woke capitalism or tribalist identity politics – a mindset that many left-wing groups adopt from right-wing movements, even if they may not be aware of it – also create such forms of regressive illusions.

The regressive element in such illusions consists precisely in the fact that those forms of expression that are based on these illusions are empty forms of expression and do not eliminate the conditions that they denounce, but rather continue to potentiate them.

Furthermore, the term regressive illusion can certainly be taken at face value, as it is always based on the assumption that there is a desirable state that never actually existed. Zygmunt Bauman has made this aspect abundantly clear, not least in his posthumously published work *Retrotopia*.[100] For Bauman, the excessive demands of the present lead to people looking for a (supposedly) better past – which, of course, never existed in this sense. For Bauman, the decisive consequence is ultimately that many people project the deficits of the present onto a past, i.e. retrotopic, tribal fire. In short: a state based on the illusion that there was once a state in which many of the problems that people are confronted with in a specific historical or social context did not exist. Freud's analysis of the phenomenon of projection in paranoid patients, however, provides a concrete indication of why such views are in fact regressive forms of illusion. For Freud, the process of projection consists in the projection of an inner discomfort/an inner state onto an exterior. Here, however, it is important to read Freud with the degree of precision he deserves. As Freud rightly points out in *Totem and Taboo*, those ghosts and demons that we perceive in the outside world are expressions of a deeper hostility:

> The hostility, of which one knows nothing and does not want to know anything, is thrown out of one's inner perception into the outside world, detached from one's own person and attributed to the other.[101]

Here, however, it is not – as in Freud's treatise – about the ceremonial which, according to Freud's reading, in primitive tribal societies ensured that one's own (unconscious hostility) towards the deceased was projected onto an external mourning ritual in order to escape punishment by the demons and metaphysical forces.[102] Concepts such as Fukuyama's idea of the *end of history* (the final victory of liberal capitalism over communism) or Putin's – seemingly retrotopian – longing for the supposedly better times of the Soviet Union, which Putin repeatedly uses to legitimise his hostility towards the decadent and individualistic West, can also be understood as such a form of projection – emerging in the form of a regressive illusion.

Duane Rousselle makes this point even clearer with regard to the recent debate between the right-wing conservative US commentator Tucker Carlson and Putin. Both Western and Russian politics find themselves in a form of regressive nostalgia, without realising that the *real* – in the best Freudian sense: the repressed – is no longer compatible with reality itself. The real, which suddenly expresses itself in the form of a regressive illusion that strives for a *return* that cannot be clearly defined, shows on the one hand that the repressed has not fully returned to consciousness, but (and this is where the danger lies) is returning as a regressive form of illusion. The West still believes in the end of history and that the principle of freedom will prevail – without being exactly clear about what the concept of freedom really means. Freedom of the economy (in the best Mileian sense) or freedom of the individual? At the same time, Putin is dreaming of a *return* to the Soviet Union. Here, too, the question remains as to what exactly the *real* is, which now appears in the form of a retrotopia that does not want to know much about the ideological foundations that explain the failure of the Soviet Union in the first place. Here, however, it is worth citing Rousselle himself, who brilliantly noted the following in a recent comment regarding the Carlson-Putin interview:

> Putin is correct that the world is changing, whether we accept it or not, and that the West is clinging to yesterday. But we can see that he is just as nostalgic as the rest of us. We are caught in a dance: we see in Putin what we deny in ourselves, and he sees in us what he denies in himself.[103]

If Rousselle assumes – I would like to grant myself this interpretative freedom at this point – that we (in the West) see in Putin what we deny in ourselves, but at the same time Putin sees in us (the West) what he denies/represses in himself, then this is a regressive rationalisation of the repressed/real that has returned, which is generated by the (political) superego. The West realises that the ideal of freedom, which was proclaimed by the end of history, is not compatible with the ideal of equality – which leads to this ideal being defended even more in order to avoid a consciousness of the repressed at all costs. At the same time, Putin also seems to realise that the repressed aspect of state socialism consists precisely in the fact that its failure can be explained by the fact that the ideal of equality has destroyed human freedom – which is why he tries to fight the latter even harder and sees the West as his main enemy. The emergence of the repressed in this context means for both the West and the Russian leaders that both ideals (freedom and equality) have never found their true realisation. Finally, it is worth recalling what Julian Assange expressed in the letter he wrote to King Charles just before his coronation. In addition to the description of the fertile conditions in Belmarsh Prison, where Assange has been imprisoned for some time, one passage from Assange's letter deserves special attention:

> On the coronation of my liege, I thought it only fitting to extend a heartfelt invitation to you to commemorate this momentous occasion by visiting your very own kingdom within a kingdom: his majesty's prison Belmarsh.[104]

The only answer – in Assange's words – is to fully admit what has been repressed, even if it may initially be traumatic. Only when we become aware that both the "End of History" and the retrotopian nostalgia for the Soviet Union are no more than regressive illusions can we pave the way for something new that lies outside these binary thought patterns. In short, we can only escape such binary patterns of thinking if we discover (become aware of) our own Belmarsh, which limits our imagination for something truly better.

References

1. Cf. Tooze, A. (2022, October 28). "Welcome to the World of the Polycrisis." *Financial Times.*
2. Ibid.
3. Ibid.
4. Cf. Marx, K. & Engels, F. (1981). *Werke (Bd.1)*, 379, Dietz: Berlin.
5. Cf. Bauman, Z. (2017). *Retrotopia.* Suhrkamp.
6. Liebelt, C. (2021, May 30). "Die AfD und ihr Normalitätsbegriff: Deutschland brutal." *Die Tageszeitung: taz.* https://taz.de/!5771233/
7. Köhler, B. (2011, May 2). "Krisen im Supermarkt. *Die Zeit.*" https://www.zeit.de/wissen/2011-05/leserartikel-garfinkel
8. Cf. Barria-Asenjo, Nicol A. (2021) *Construcción de Una Nueva Normalidad. Notas Sobre un Chile Pandémico.* Madrid: Psimática.
9. Wessollek, M. & dpa. (2023, November 12). "Verteidigungspolitik: Boris Pistorius verteidigt seine Forderung nach Kriegstüchtigkeit." *Die Zeit.* https://www.zeit.de/politik/2023-11/bundeswehr-boris-pistorius-verteidigungspolitik-kriegstuechtigkeit (translated to English).
10. Ibid.
11. *The Project Gutenberg ebook of Jenseits des Lustprinzips, by Sigmund Freud.* Retrieved February 18, 2024, from https://www.gutenberg.org/files/28220/28220-h/28220-h.htm
12. *Sigmund Freud: Das Unbehagen in der Kultur.* Retrieved February 18, 2024, from https://www.projekt-gutenberg.org/freud/unbehag/unbehag.html
13. Cf. Einstein, A. & Freud, S. (1972). *Warum Krieg?.* Zürich. Diogenes Verlag. https://ittybyte.files.wordpress.com/

2015/03/einstein-albert-warum-krieg.pdf (nonpaginated, translated to English).

14. Ibid.

15. Ibid.

16. Ibid.

17. *Even in Argentina's Poorest Neighborhoods, Far-Right Javier Milei Is Gaining Ground.* Retrieved February 18, 2024, from https://jacobin.com/2023/10/argentina-far-right-javier-milei-villa-31-us-dollar-working-class.

18. *IN FULL: Argentina President Javier Milei's Inauguration Address.* (n.d.). Retrieved February 18, 2024, from https://www.youtube.com/watch?v=sHqM5ClXh00

19. Callison, W. (2023, October 15). The Anarcho-Authoritarianism of Javier Milei. *Latinoamérica 21.* https://latinoamerica21.com/en/the-anarcho-authoritarianism-of-javier-milei/

20. "Argentina Elects Far-Right, Chainsaw-Wielding Javier Milei as President," (2023, November 20). *Politico.* https://www.politico.eu/article/argentina-elects-a-far-right-chainsaw-wielding-president/.

21. Amlinger, C. & Nachtwey, O. (2022). *Gekränkte Freiheit. Aspekte des Libertären Autoritarismus.* 3rd. Edition. Berlin: Suhrkamp. (translated to English).

22. Ibid., p.17

23. "Cinco Definiciones Fuertes de Javier Milei: Armas, Drogas, Homosexualidad, Aborto y el Estado como Enemigo." (2021, August 9). https://www.cronista.com/economia-politica/cinco-definiciones-fuertes-de-javier-milei-aborto-drogas-armas-homosexualidad-y-el-estado-enemigo/

24. Lutz, D. / S. (2023, November 20). "Argentina's next president says it's ok to sell babies—Here's why bitcoin lovers love him." Decrypt. https://decrypt.co/206724/argentina-next-president-says-ok-sell-babies-why-bitcoin-lovers-love-him

25. "Milei mobilisiert den Unmut einer neuen informellen Arbeiterschaft." (2023, December 20). *Jacobin Magazine.* https://jacobin.de/artikel/javier-milei-argentinien-arbeiterklasse

26. Amlinger, C. & Nachtwey, O. (2022). *Gekränkte Freiheit. Aspekte des Libertären Autoritarismus,* 11, 3rd. Edition. Berlin: Suhrkamp. (translated to English).

27. Cf. Žižek, S. (2023). *Freedom – A Disease Without Cure.* London: Bloomsbury.

28. Ibid., pp. 18–19.

29. Ibid., p. 19.

30. "The End of Progressive Neoliberalism." *Dissent Magazine.* Accessed March 4, 2024. https://www.dissentmagazine.org/online_articles/progressive-neoliberalism-reactionary-populism-nancy-fraser/.

31. "Courtiers and Sycophants: Catherine Liu's Case Against the Professional Managerial Class," July 20, 2021. *Los Angeles Review of Books.* https://lareviewofbooks.org/article/courtiers-and-sycophants-catherine-lius-case-against-the-professional-managerial-class.

32. Cf. Diversität bei Amazon. (2018, April 16). DE About Amazon. https://www.aboutamazon.de/news/diversitaet-chancengleicheit-und-inklusion/diversitaet-bei-amazon. (translated to English).

33. Glamazon: So geht vielfalt! (2018, March 9). DE About Amazon. https://www.aboutamazon.de/news/diversitaet-chancengleicheit-und-inklusion/glamazon-so-geht-vielfalt. (translated to English).

34. "Amazon und der Psychoterror." (2021, April 30). https://www.ipg-journal.de/rubriken/arbeit-und-digitalisierung/artikel/amazon-usa-5128/

35. Cf. Jones, O. (2019, May 23). "Woke-washing: How brands are cashing in on the culture wars." *The Guardian.*

https://www.theguardian.com/media/2019/may/23/woke-washing-brands-cashing-in-on-culture-wars-owen-jones

36. Opinion I are crazed commies running american corporations? I common dreams. (n.d.). Retrieved October 30, 2023, from https://www.commondreams.org/views/2021/06/10/are-crazed-commies-running-american-corporations

37. Cf. Marx, K. & Engels, F. (1981). *Werke (Bd.1)*, 379, Dietz: Berlin.

38. Wirtz, M. (2019). "Überlebensirrtum im Dorsch lexikon der Psychologie." https://dorsch.hogrefe.com/stichwort/ueberlebensirrtum

39. Reshe, Julie (2020). "Depressive realism – We keep chasing happiness, but true clarity comes from depression and existential angst. Admit that life is hell, and be free." https://aeon.co/essays/the-voice-of-sadness-is-censored-as-sick-what-if-its-sane

40. Fromm, Erich (2020). *Jenseits der Illusionen: Eine Intellektuelle Autobiographie.* Munich: Deutscher Taschenbuch-Verlag, 98. (Tranlated to English).

41. Hahn, D. (2021, January 2). "Auslieferung von Julian Assange: Hoffen auf Gnade." *Die Tageszeitung: taz.* https://taz.de/!5736388/

42. "Skandalprozess in London: Dramatischer Kampf um das Leben von Julian Assange." (n.d.). *Der Standard.* Retrieved October 30, 2023, from https://www.derstandard.de/story/2000121079416/skandalprozess-in-london-dramatischer-kampf-um-das-leben-von-julian

43. Fromm, E. (2005). "Haben oder Sein: Die seelischen Grundlagen einer neuen Gesellschaft," 98, dtv.

44. Cárdenas, M. (2022, June 16). "Today's Crises are Different by Mauricio Cárdenas." Project Syndicate. https://www.project-syndicate.org/commentary/new-

generation-of-crises-global-public-goods-by-mauricio-cardenas-2022-06

45. Chaudhury, D. R. (2022, June 4). "India not sitting on fence, entitled to have its own side: S Jaishankar on Russia-Ukraine war." *The Economic Times*. https://economictimes. indiatimes.com/news/india/india-not-sitting-on-fence-entitled-to-have-its-own-side-s-jaishankar-on-russia-ukraine-war/articleshow/91993466.cms

46. Schumann, D. F., & Arzt, I. (2021, November 15). Weltgesundheitsorganisation: "Die Pandemie wird enden, wenn wir es wollen." *Die Zeit*. https://www.zeit. de/gesundheit/2021-11/who-mike-ryan-corona-pandemie-epidemiologe-corona-impfung

47. El-Erian, M. A. (2022, May 13). "Beware a global economy with little fires everywhere by mohamed a. El-erian." Project Syndicate. https://www.project-syndicate.org/ commentary/ukraine-war-economic-consequences-for-developing-countries-by-mohamed-a-el-erian-2022-05

48. Burgis, B. (2022, March 17). "Is 'Whataboutism' Always a Bad Thing?" *Current Affairs*. https://www.currentaffairs. org/2022/03/is-whataboutism-always-a-bad-thing

49. Bogost, I. (2022, December 7). "ChatGPT Is Dumber Than You Think." *The Atlantic*. https://www.theatlantic.com/ technology/archive/2022/12/chatgpt-openai-artificial-intelligence-writing-ethics/672386/

50. Pfaller, R. (2018). *Interpassivity: The Aesthetics of Delegated Enjoyment*, 50, Edinburgh University Press.

51. Bauman, Zygmunt. Socialism: *The Active Utopia. Controversies in Sociology: 3*. London: Allen and Unwin, 13, 1976.

52. Tewari, A. (2023, February 22). "I Chat, therefore I am!" *Sublation Magazine*. https://www.sublationmag.com/post/ i-chat-therefore-i-am

53. Rosselli, C. (2017). *Liberal Socialism* (N. Urbinati, Ed.; W. McCuaig, Trans.), 61, Princeton University Press.
54. Ibid.
55. Pfaller, R. (2018). *Interpassivity: The Aesthetics of Delegated Enjoyment*, 50, Edinburgh University Press.
56. Bauman, Z. (1976). *Socialism: The Active Utopia*, 13, Allen and Unwin.
57. Bown, A. (2018). *Interpassive Online: Outsourcing and Insourcing Enjoyment in Platform Capitalism*, 323. https://doi.org/10.26021/230
58. Van Oenen, G. (2011). "Interpassive Agency: Engaging Actor-network-Theory's View on the Agency of Objects." *Theory & Event*, 14(2). https://doi.org/10.1353/tae.2011.0014
59. Ibid. 10–11
60. Ibid.
61. Turchin, A. (manuscript). "Message to Any Future AI: 'There Are Several Instrumental Reasons Why Exterminating Humanity Is Not in Your Interest.'" https://philarchive.org/rec/TURMTA
62. *Erich Fromm on Disobedience*. (n.d.). Retrieved October 30, 2023, from http://eqi.org/erich_fromm_on_disobedience.htm.
63. *Krieg und Empörung*. Süddeutsche.de. Retrieved March 4, 2024, from https://www.sueddeutsche.de/projekte/artikel/kultur/das-dilemma-des-westens-juergen-habermas-zum-krieg-in-der-ukraine-e068321/ (translated to English).
64. With regard to the previous statements, see my argumentation in an article published for *The European*: https://www.theeuropean.de/gesellschaft-kultur/putin-und-die-atomare-bedrohung
65. Deutschlandfunk.de. (n.d.). *Europa-gipfel in granada—Scholz will mit nein zu taurus eskalation vermeiden*. Die Nachrichten. Retrieved March 4, 2024, from https://www.

deutschlandfunk.de/scholz-will-mit-nein-zu-taurus-eskalation-vermeiden-100.html

66. *Krieg und Empörung*. Süddeutsche.de. Retrieved March 4, 2024, from https://www.sueddeutsche.de/projekte/artikel/kultur/das-dilemma-des-westens-juergen-habermas-zum-krieg-in-der-ukraine-e068321/ (translated to English).

67. Ibid.

68. *Putins Rechnung geht auf*. (2023, December 12). https://www.akweb.de/politik/ukraine-krieg-putins-rechnung-geht-auf/

69. Studebaker, B. (2023, June 27). "Revolution Without the Risks: Enjoying the Adventures of Yevgeny Prigozhin." *Sublation Magazine*. https://www.sublationmag.com/post/revolution-without-the-risks-enjoying-the-adventures-of-yevgeny-prigozhin

70. Ibid.

71. "Dr Jordan Peterson – The Postmodernist Drinking Song." Retrieved November 5, 2023, from https://genius.com/Dr-jordan-b-peterson-the-postmodernist-drinking-song-lyrics

72. Peterson, J. B., Doidge, N., & Van Sciver, E. (2019). *12 Rules for Life: An Antidote to Chaos*. Penguin Books, 147 ff.

73. "Postmodernism: Definition and Critique (With a few comments on its relationship with Marxism) – Jordan Peterson." (n.d.). Retrieved November 5, 2023, from https://www.jordanbpeterson.com/philosophy/postmodernism-definition-and-critique-with-a-few-comments-on-its-relationship-with-marxism/

74. Cf. ibid.

75. Ibid.

76. "Jordan Peterson's 'Postmodern Neomarxism' Is Pure Hokum." (n.d.). Retrieved November 5, 2023, from https://

jacobin.com/2022/03/jordan-peterson-postmodernism-marxism-philosophy-zizek

77. Ibid.

78. "Postmodernism: Definition and Critique (With a few comments on its relationship with Marxism) – Jordan Peterson." (n.d.). Retrieved November 5, 2023, from https://www.jordanbpeterson.com/philosophy/postmodernism-definition-and-critique-with-a-few-comments-on-its-relationship-with-marxism/

79. Cf. Ibid.

80. Ibid.

81. Cf. ibid.

82. Cf. ibid.

83. Ibid.

84. "Jordan Peterson's 'Postmodern Neomarxism Is Pure Hokum." (n.d.). Retrieved November 5, 2023, from https://jacobin.com/2022/03/jordan-peterson-postmodernism-marxism-philosophy-zizek

85. Erich Fromm Glossary – Grundbegriffe Erich Fromms. https://fromm-online.org/wp-content/uploads/glossar/115-273.pdf#

86. Cf. ibid.

87. Ibid.

88. Stark, M. (2023, February 11). Liebe: Warum sind wir eigentlich nicht zusammen? *Die Zeit.* https://www.zeit.de/2023/07/liebe-philosophie-georg-friedrich-wilhelm-hegel

89. McGowan, T. (2018). *Hegel in Love. Can Philosophy Love? Reflections and Encounters, 4,* Eds. Cindy Zeiher and Todd McGowan (London: Rowman and Littlefield, 2018). Retrieved March 5, 2024, from https://www.academia.edu/36591051/Hegel_in_Love

90. Breithaupt, F., & Hamilton, A. B. B. (2019). *The dark sides of empathy*. Cornell University Press. https://www.jstor.org/stable/10.7591/j.ctvfc5436

91. Ibid., p. 222.

92. Maiwald, F. (2022, October 27). "The Burden of Freedom: Sartre's Sleep and Fromm's Awakening." *Epoché Magazine*. https://epochemagazine.org/56/the-burden-of-freedom-sartres-sleep-and-fromms-awakening/.

93. *Communist manifesto (Chapter 2)*. (n.d.). Retrieved March 5, 2024, from https://www.marxists.org/archive/marx/works/1848/communist-manifesto/ch02.htm.

94. Adorno, T. W., & Adorno, T. W. (1951). *Minima Moralia: Reflexionen aus dem beschädigten Leben*, 480, Frankfurt am Main: Suhrkamp. (translated to English).

95. Sona, R. (2006). *Der Begriff des Glücks bei Adorno. Kritiknetz. de* https://www.kritiknetz.de/images/stories/texte/Der_Begriff_des_Gluecks_bei_Adorno.pdf

96. Feldman, D. (2023, November 13). "Germany is a good place to be Jewish. Unless, like me, you're a Jew who criticises Israel." *The Guardian*. https://www.theguardian.com/commentisfree/2023/nov/13/germany-jewish-criticise-israel-tv-debate

97. Butler, J. (2023, October 13). "The Compass of Mourning." *London Review of Books*, 45(20). https://www.lrb.co.uk/the-paper/v45/n20/judith-butler/the-compass-of-mourning

98. Blome, T. (2023, December 9). Selbstbetrug: Wenn man mal ehrlich ist, sollte man sich selbst belügen. *Die Zeit*. https://www.zeit.de/kultur/2023-12/selbsterkenntnis-selbstbetrug-delulu

99. Cf. Marx, K. & Engels, F. (1981). *Werke (Bd.1)*, 379, Dietz: Berlin.

100. Cf. Bauman, Z. (2017). *Retrotopia*. Suhrkamp.

101. Freud, S. (1940) *Gesammelte Werke. Neunter Band. Totem und Tabu.* London: Imago Publishing Co., p. 79, Ltd. (translated to English).
102. Cf. ibid., p. 80.
103. Rousselle,D. (2024, February 11). "The Future Is Stupid." *Medium.* https://duanerousselle.medium.com/the-future-is-stupid-ebf2185cbf1a
104. Cassidy, C. (2023, May 6). "Julian Assange Writes Letter to King Charles and Urges Him to Visit Belmarsh Prison." *The Guardian.* https://www.theguardian.com/media/2023/may/06/julian-assange-writes-letter-to-king-charles-and-urges-him-to-visit-belmarsh-prison.

Framespotting
Changing how you look at things changes how you see them
Laurence & Alison Matthews
A punchy, upbeat guide to framespotting. Spot deceptions
and hidden assumptions; swap growth for growing up.
See and be free.
Paperback: 978-1-78279-689-3 ebook: 978-1-78279-822-4

Is There an Afterlife?
David Fontana
Is there an Afterlife? If so what is it like? How do
Western ideas of the afterlife compare with Eastern?
David Fontana presents the historical and contemporary
evidence for survival of physical death.
Paperback: 978-1-90381-690-5

Nothing Matters
a book about nothing
Ronald Green
Thinking about Nothing opens the world to
everything by illuminating new angles to old problems
and stimulating new ways of thinking.
Paperback: 978-1-84694-707-0 ebook: 978-1-78099-016-3

Panpsychism
The Philosophy of the Sensuous Cosmos
Peter Ells
Are free will and mind chimeras? This book, anti-
materialistic but respecting science, answers: No!
Mind is foundational to all existence.
Paperback: 978-1-84694-505-2 ebook: 978-1-78099-018-7

Punk Science
Inside the Mind of God
Manjir Samanta-Laughton
Many have experienced unexplainable phenomena; God,
psychic abilities, extraordinary healing and angelic encounters.
Can cutting-edge science actually explain phenomena
previously thought of as 'paranormal'?
Paperback: 978-1-90504-793-2

The Vagabond Spirit of Poetry
Edward Clarke
Spend time with the wisest poets of the modern age and
of the past, and let Edward Clarke remind you of the
importance of poetry in our industrialized world.
Paperback: 978-1-78279-370-0 ebook: 978-1-78279-369-4

Readers of ebooks can buy or view any of these bestsellers by
clicking on the live link in the title. Most titles are published in
paperback and as an ebook. Paperbacks are available in traditional
bookshops. Both print and ebook formats are available online.
Find more titles and sign up to our readers' newsletter at
www.collectiveinkbooks.com/non-fiction
Follow us on Facebook at
www.facebook.com/CINonFiction

of conceptual mediations, effectively supported by the most authoritative bibliography, to reveal the ideological plot of the current movement towards barbarism that we experience in our present. Critical of both classical Marxism and hegemonic post-structuralism, Maiwald shows us how the same capitalism that destroys the entire civilizing process only has to commercialise the barbarism of an impossible concept of happiness, which can only be imagined through regressive illusions. Endowed with a diaphanous clarity and a pleasant elegance, Maiwald offers us an x-ray of the central elements of our world, while making a precise commitment to recover an emancipatory subject.

José Luis Villacañas, author of *Populismo*

In *Regressive Illusions*, Florian Maiwald performs the critical work of exposing and exploring the perennial contradictions of the capitalist market that is at all times at pains to mystify. In today's context, bad faith promises of "freedom" – emptied of their emancipatory possibility via commodity logic – have come to disguise the very mechanisms by which we are always more captured by the oppositional, exploitative and reactionary impetuses of the market. In this context, obfuscatory promises that align with capitalist logic have perhaps ushered in a "socialism", but one that exists only for the corporate and billionaire classes. For the masses, commodity logic has extended even to subjectivity and surplus value is being generated for a monopoly class via labour that is not even recognised as such. There is a further crisis of redistribution, where profits are guarded by tax breaks, grants, subsidies and short-term incentives. In *Regressive Illusions*, Maiwald abandons neutered interpretations of original thinkers that have come to serve these regressive workings of the market. He returns, brilliantly, to the radical – and often necessarily contradictory – core of writers such as Marx, Hegel, Adorno and Habermas, reinterpreting today's difficult context in light of their philosophical work. Ultimately, Maiwald reminds us that "there is no revolution without self-love" – an urgent reminder when depression, rage and utopianism have seemingly obliterated the political and facilitated an ever-expanding Bad Infinity towards the commoditisation and ruination of everything: our selves, our relationships, the very future of our world.

Helen Rollins, author of *Psychocinema*